Organic Gardening Techniques

Nick Hamilton

Organic Gardening Techniques

CompanionHouse Books™ is an imprint of Fox Chapel Publishers International Ltd.

Project Team
Vice President-Content: Christopher Reggio
Editor: Amy Deputato/Jeremy Hauck
Copy Editor: Anthony Regolino
Design: Mary Ann Kahn
Index: Elizabeth Walker

ISBN 978-1-62008-273-7

Library of Congress Cataloging-in-Publication Data

Names: Hamilton, Nick, author.
Title: Organic gardening techniques : the guide to planting, growing, and
  care of your fruits, vegetables, and herbs / by Nick Hamilton.
Description: Mount Joy, PA : Fox Chapel Publishing, [2018] | Includes index.
  Identifiers: LCCN 2017058057 (print) | LCCN 2017061469 (ebook) | ISBN
  9781620082744 (ebook) | ISBN 9781620082737 (softcover)
Subjects: LCSH: Organic gardening.
Classification: LCC SB453.5 (ebook) | LCC SB453.5 .H3653 2018 (print) | DDC
  635.9/87--dc23
LC record available at https://lccn.loc.gov/2017058057

Fox Chapel Publishing
903 Square Street
Mount Joy, PA 17552

Fox Chapel Publishers International Ltd.
7 Danefield Road, Selsey (Chichester)
West Sussex PO20 9DA, U.K.

www.facebook.com/companionhousebooks

We are always looking for talented authors. To submit an idea, please send a brief inquiry to acquisitions@foxchapelpublishing.com.

Printed and bound in Singapore
21 20 19 18   2 4 6 8 10 9 7 5 3 1

Contents

Introduction

The art of producing an excellent and abundant harvest year after year comes down to two simple things: employing the best techniques to achieve your goal and knowing all there is to know about the crop you are growing. Many of these techniques are tried-and-tested methods that have been used, almost unchanged, for centuries—not because nobody has come up with a better method, but because they actually work. If you talk to any experienced professional grower or community-garden user, it soon becomes apparent that every grower, professional or amateur, in every region, has a slightly different way of achieving the same result. Therefore, the methods explained in this book are very much guidelines and, although most will work for the majority of gardeners without any modifications, some techniques will require tweaking in order to suit the area, the style of growing, the soil, and so on.

The most important part of growing any productive crop is to start planning and preparing for the next one at the end of each season. This is why the book begins with the basics—the planning and the tools required in order to grow fruit and vegetables productively. Knowing the basics is more important than knowing sowing dates, varieties, or potential size of harvest. If the basics are not right, then neither will be the harvest.

Once the plans have been put into place and the tools prepared for the season ahead, the various techniques for producing bountiful harvests throughout the season, as well as out of season, can be implemented. All of these techniques have been used at Barnsdale, with many beginning life as completely different techniques that were modified and tweaked in order to get the best out of individual crops. I believe that pushing the boundaries as far as crop production is concerned is vital in an organic garden. In this way, you can make the most of the space available and produce a continuous supply of fruit and vegetables that would keep any gardener, novice or experienced, out of his or her local supermarket. This starts with the propagation of crops, both indoors and out, which will invariably dictate not only the size but also the timing of our harvests.

When it comes to fruit, it seems that most gardeners struggle with pruning and training, but it is not as complicated as it may seem at the outset. Each year at

Barnsdale, we are able to harvest an abundance of soft as well as tree fruit using the simple training and pruning methods explained in this book.

I find pests and diseases fascinating—not because I like to see them, but because it is one of those battles in life that swings one way, then the next, with every growing season, having an unknown outcome. Fortunately, the organic gardener can win that battle most years, using very simple techniques, and end up with near-perfect fruit and vegetables while filling the garden with the fantastic sound of abundant wildlife. The sound of birdsong and the buzzing of insects will not be disturbed by the drone of a freezer, because this book shows you how to store fruit and vegetables in a way that can keep some crops available for use in the kitchen all year round.

The joy of gardening is in the doing, and that means not only being in the productive garden as often as is required or possible but also cobbling together the necessary equipment needed to run a productive area successfully. There are plenty of things that anybody who is able to wield a hammer and saw can easily construct. I hope this book will give every gardener the information, confidence, and encouragement required to get out into the garden and grow fruit and vegetables using techniques that are uncomplicated, simple, and effective—and really work.

Barnsdale and the Hamiltons

Geoff Hamilton's passion for gardening led him to earn a National Diploma in horticulture from Writtle Agricultural College in Essex, UK, in 1959. From there, as his passion, knowledge, and skills grew, he went on to create a garden center, write for gardening publications, and appear on gardening-related television shows. In the mid-1970s, Geoff and his family (including three sons, Stephen, Christopher, and Nicholas, the latter of whom is the author of this book) were living in a house on the Barnsdale Hall estate and gardening on rented land when Geoff was asked to appear on the BBC's *Gardener's World* and soon landed a permanent spot on the television show. Wanting more room for his gardening endeavors, he relocated to a home with 5 acres of land just a short way from the "original" Barnsdale, and Barnsdale Gardens were born. Barnsdale's thirty-eight individual gardens showcase Geoff's pioneering work in organic gardening, and his vision is carried on today by a second generation of gardening Hamiltons. (See pages 200–207 for more about Barnsdale Gardens.)

Chapter 1

Planning and Preparing for Your Garden

Planning and Rotating Crops

Crop rotation is a subject that often causes confusion, both in terms of its importance to the vegetable grower and what crops are involved. It is a practice that is primarily used in the cultivation of vegetables, and in an ideal world, we would all have a garden that could be easily divided into four equal and adequately sized areas where we could grow all the vegetables we require. Unfortunately, we do not all necessarily have the right setup. The recommendations given are therefore to be viewed as the ideal, but they are not set in stone. Individual gardeners can do only the best they can in their individual situations, which is often not the perfect scenario.

Why Rotate Crops?

There are two main reasons for rotating crops; both apply to a situation in which the same crop is grown in the same place year after year. The first reason is to help in the control of pests and diseases, while the second concerns the nutrient levels of the soil. If the same crop is grown on the same piece of ground year after year, the likelihood that the crop will become badly infected with pests or diseases specific to that crop is vastly increased. Moving the crop each year prevents a buildup of soil-borne pests and diseases that may affect each crop grown. Most of these pests and diseases will not last in the ground long enough to reinfect the crop when it is grown there again.

The grouping of plants is critical, as each group will contain plants that suffer from similar pests and diseases and also have similar nutrient requirements. Therefore, to avoid a crop being infected with a pest or disease specific to that type, there should not be a similar crop from the same group coming onto that plot in the following year. If you are implementing a four-year crop rotation, the groups are as follows:

Group 1	Group 2	Group 3	Group 4
cabbage	green (runner) bean	cucumber	carrot
broccoli	French bean	squash	beet (beetroot)
Chinese cabbage	pea	pumpkin	parsnip
brussels sprout	fava (broad) bean	melon	scorzonera
cauliflower	lima bean	potato	salsify
kale	sweet corn	tomato	Hamburg parsley
rutabaga (swede)	okra	summer squash (marrow)	celeriac
turnip	globe artichoke	zucchini (courgette)	onion
radish	lettuce	eggplant (aubergine)	shallot
kohlrabi	endive	pepper	leek
	chicory		garlic
	cress		celery
			Florence fennel
			spinach
			chard

To minimize possible reinfection, a four-year crop rotation is the ideal solution. This involves dividing the vegetable plot into four equal parts, so that in the first year one of each of the crop groups can be grown in each plot. In the second year, each group is moved around to the next plot, then the same move again in the third year, and so on, so that in the fifth year all the groups are in the plots in which they originally started during year 1. The cycle then starts all over again.

If permanent crops are also being grown, such as soft fruit or rhubarb, these can be kept in a completely separate area and the four-year plan rotated around them. An alternative option would be to incorporate the permanent crops into your plan so that each group is rotated only over a three-year period, as one of the plots will be permanent. This would alter the vegetables into the following groups:

Group 1	Group 2	Group 3	
cabbage	green (runner) bean	cucumber	parsnip
broccoli	French bean	squash	scorzonera
Chinese cabbage	pea	pumpkin	salsify
brussels sprout	fava (broad) bean	melon	Hamburg parsley
cauliflower	lima bean	potato	celeriac
kale	sweet corn	tomato	onion
rutabaga (swede)	okra	summer squash (marrow)	shallot
turnip	globe artichoke	zucchini (courgette)	leek
radish	lettuce	eggplant (aubergine)	garlic
kohlrabi	endive	pepper	celery
	chicory	carrot	Florence fennel
	cress	beet (beetroot)	
	spinach		
	chard		

As you can see, Group 4 is divided between Groups 2 and 3.

Catch Crops

These vegetable groups should be used as a fairly accurate guide, but not as an unalterable list. With the longer-maturing crops, such as cabbages, broccoli, kale, and potatoes, it is possible to grow what are called "catch crops" between them. These crops may be from a different vegetable group to the one being grown, but their pest and disease implications will be negligible as they are quick-maturing crops and are harvested before they can affect the growth of the main crop. A catch crop does not have to fit into the crop rotation plan, as it is in the ground for such a short space of time that its impact is minimal, although its inclusion should always be in the overall growing plan. Catch crops can be vegetables such as lettuce, radish, scallion (green onion), arugula (rocket), spinach, and a host of mini or baby vegetable varieties as well as multi-sown onions, beet (beetroot), leek, carrot, turnip, and kohlrabi.

Planning Your Crops

It is important during the cold winter months to sit back with a pile of seed catalogs and plan what is to be grown in the season ahead. This will ensure that all the productive ground is utilized to its best potential and that maximum cropping is achieved. The overall plan of where crops will be planted in the vegetable area and how much needs to be grown—as well as which crops will follow once one has been harvested—must also fit with the space allocated for each group of vegetables within the crop rotation plan. If this all sounds somewhat complicated and confusing at this stage, it is nothing compared to the potential mayhem caused by not knowing what to plant where, which crop should follow the one just harvested, and ending up with an overabundance of one vegetable that you cannot use.

It is important first to look at the space available and divide it into four equal parts so that the best crop rotation can be implemented. Next, sit down and look at the available crops for each section before deciding what to grow. There may be an excellent source of organic fruit and vegetables to buy in your locality and hence no need to take up valuable space growing vegetables that are cheap to buy when the more expensive or less easy-to-obtain vegetables could be grown in that space instead. Why grow a garden full of cheap-to-buy organic potatoes and then buy overpriced corn, cucumbers, and tomatoes from the supermarket?

The next concern is to ensure that all of the crops do not mature at once. My philosophy is "little and often" where vegetables are concerned. If I have allocated a row of carrots in the roots area of the productive garden, I never sow the complete row all at once. In this way, the carrots mature at a nice even rate and can be harvested fresh and sweet. They will not have to sit in the ground, waiting until they are needed, where they may become tough, corky, and tasteless. I like to apply this principle to most vegetables I grow. An exception is the fruiting vegetables that just keep producing their harvest throughout the season, such as tomatoes, melons, cucumbers,

Radishes can serve as a quick catch crop between longer-maturing crops.

Sowing and harvesting a crop at different times ensures a constant supply of fresh vegetables.

peppers, eggplant (aubergine), summer squash (marrow), zucchini (courgette), and the like. Green (runner), French, and fava (broad) beans, however, can be manipulated so that their crops also extend over a longer season. This is done by planting early and following with two more plantings, one as a main crop and one to follow at the end of the main-crop season. This usually means we can have green (runner) and French beans from the end of June right through until the end of October.

Vegetable growing is most certainly not just about tossing a few seeds in and harvesting when they mature. To do it successfully, it is important to plan sufficiently, allowing for the odd disaster along the way that may alter the plan slightly. Again, this is the ideal, but flexibility is also essential to getting things right.

The Right Tools for the Job

Long gone are the days when we have to use our hands for every job in the productive garden. Mind you, I always find it very satisfying to finish my time on the vegetable plot with dirty hands. Even if you haven't done a lot of manual work, it always feels as if your time has been well spent.

Over the years, there has been a tool or piece of equipment developed to make every job in the garden that much easier. There will always be certain items that are reserved only for technophiles or gardeners who just have to have everything, regardless of whether they are really all that useful. Most gardeners swear by the tools and equipment they have had for years, but modern developments in certain areas have made gardening much easier, so the best range of tools is a mix between the two.

Essential Tools
Spade

If asked to name one tool for use in the productive garden, I would think that most gardeners would give "spade" as the answer. Soil cultivation is one of the most essential constituents in the productive process, and the spade is the workhorse most used to satisfy this requirement. There are two basic types, the border spade and the digging (or garden) spade. Although named for use in other areas of the garden, the border spade does have a place in some growers' sheds, particularly those who have a bad back, limited mobility, or just find a digging spade too heavy to handle when full of soil. The better the quality of the spade, the more expensive it will be, but also the longer it will last. For that reason, I always look toward wooden-handled border and digging spades.

There is a spade out there for everyone, as different makes will result in different lengths of handle. There is no substitute for going to the garden center and trying out a prospective spade in person. This will limit the problem of backache caused by using an inappropriate piece of equipment. Breaking or losing a trusty spade can be likened to a pool player breaking his cue or a golfer losing his trusty putter! My preference

A spade with a wooden handle can withstand heavy-duty use.

is for a stainless-steel blade on my spade, primarily because we have a clay soil at Barnsdale, and I find that it is much easier to dig with this type of blade.

The digging spade has a larger blade and therefore stronger handle than the border spade, as it is made for heavier work. Both types will need to be treated with respect to ensure that the blade is not damaged or the handle broken. The great advantage of wooden-handled types is that, after many years of use, when the spade has more than fulfilled the promise shown on that first day and the handle finally snaps, you can buy a new handle to replace the broken one. This is not possible with plastic handles.

If you are going to be doing a lot of digging, it may be worthwhile investing in a spade that has a foot tread on the blade. It is very easy to get into the digging groove and, without thinking, end up with a hole in the bottom of a good pair of boots because the corner of the spade has pierced it. This generally happens when pushing into heavier ground, but if this may be a problem, then a spade with a foot tread is the answer. It will spread the weight on the underside of the foot and prevent the spade from piercing any quality boot.

The versatile garden fork has a wide range of uses.

Fork

The same principles apply to forks as do to spades with regard to the quality bought and the length of handle required. I use my fork for light cultivation of the soil, as well as for breaking up the bottom of the trench when double-digging. A fork is used for many more jobs than a spade, although not usually for such heavy work. It can be used for cultivating, breaking up lumpy soil, harvesting root crops, dividing large clumps of herbs and artichokes, and filling wheelbarrows with organic matter, as well as many other jobs in the ornamental garden. There are also border forks as well as the digging fork, with the border forks having a smaller head. These are useful for gardeners who cannot manage the larger digging forks.

Spork

This is a hybrid between a spade and a fork, hence the name. It does a job that is somewhere between the two, as the tines are wider than a standard fork, but it does not have a complete blade like a spade.

For gardeners confined to a wheelchair or with limited mobility, this tool is easier to use than a spade, but moves more soil than a standard fork.

Trowel

Trowels are usually sold in sets with small forks. I find the trowel essential in the productive garden, but not so the fork, which seems to disappear off into the ornamental garden area. The trowel is primarily used when planting or transplanting crops outside,

Trowels and small forks work well for more precise work.

although it can also be used to divide smaller clumps of herbs, where a spade or fork would be just too large. Along with the dibble, this is probably the most likely tool to be lost or inadvertently damaged.

Trowels also work well as measuring sticks, so, depending on which crop is being planted, using the trowel will very often save on having to fetch the planting board. There is also an easy-grip trowel available, where a soft-grip handle is angled approximately 90 degrees from the trowel blade.

Dibble

Essentially, the dibble is a tool for making a long hole in which to sow large seed, such as fava (broad) beans or green (runner) beans, or plant vegetables. There are types that have markings down their length that are very useful when determining at what depth the appropriate seed is being sown. Although dibbles make excellent presents, if you do not want to go to that expense for yourself, they are cheap and simple to make. (See instructions on page 199.)

A dibble is used to make holes for sowing seeds or transplanting seedlings.

Rake

The garden rake is a must for leveling ground and preparing seedbeds, but is also one of the most dangerous tools in the garden shed. It is so easy to lay it down in between jobs, forget where you put it, and then cause severe facial damage to yourself or somebody else when you inadvertently stand on the rake head. When not in use, rakes should always be left with the head up and the end of the handle on the ground. It is better still to hang them up in a toolshed or cupboard.

The head of the rake comprises usually between eight and fifteen prongs. Rakes are available with varying gaps between each prong, with everybody having a particular favorite dependent on their soil type, what they want their rake to achieve, and their or a family member's or friend's past experience. It is possible to buy metal, wooden, or plastic rakes to fit the requirement. When raking soil, the rake head will collect large soil clumps and stones but allow the majority of soil to pass through.

Long-Handled Hoe

There are two main types of long-handled hoe: the draw hoe and the Dutch hoe. It is beneficial to have one of each in the shed, with the Dutch hoe being used for weeding and the draw hoe mainly for making furrows.

In the organic productive garden, weeds should usually be small and therefore young and soft when they are hoed off, so the Dutch hoe, which is pushed forward

The long-handled Dutch hoe is helpful for weeding.

to cut off the top of the weeds where they meet the soil,
is very easy and efficient at the job. The draw hoe is very good
for chopping through larger, woodier weeds, as a sharp downward action
will usually do the job. I find that the draw hoe also moves quite a lot of soil around
during weeding, while the soil falls through the large central hole of a Dutch hoe,
leaving the soil very much in place.

Onion Hoe

The much smaller handheld onion hoe is used where the other types of hoe would be
too cumbersome, so it is ideal for hoeing weeds growing in between plants growing
in rows.

Wheelbarrow

There will always be material that has to be moved around the productive areas, and
there is no better piece of equipment for this task than the wheelbarrow. In an organic
garden, the wheelbarrow will transport mostly soil, compost, or farmyard manure. For
tiny vegetable areas, a bucket may suffice, but most people will find a wheelbarrow
essential.

As with most tools, there are several
different makes, each having good points
and bad, with each being preferred by
some gardeners, while others will like
another type. The only comment I would
make is to look for a wheelbarrow that
has an inflatable rubber tire. Although
there may be the odd puncture to repair,
pushing heavy loads, such as organic
matter or soil, will be made much
easier with this type of wheel. The most
satisfying use of a wheelbarrow is when
you have to use it to bring the harvest
from the productive garden to the house.

Hammer

Apart from the obvious hammering in of nails when building structures such as compost bins, a hammer is handy for smashing items such as brassica stems before they are put into the compost bin.

Tape Measure

If you do not have a planting board, then a tape measure is the next best thing to use in ensuring that your row and plant spacing is correct.

Planting Board

A planting board is used for measuring the distance between rows and the planting distances of various vegetable crops and herbs. As we have 4-foot (120-cm) beds dotted about the various gardens at Barnsdale, this is the obvious length to have our planting board. That said, it is an easy length to use and carry around the garden, and a planting board is very easy to make. (See instructions on page 192.)

Planks

For anybody growing on a heavy clay soil, planks are imperative if work is to be carried out in the winter. The planks will spread the weight of both heavy wheelbarrows and a person, thereby reducing compaction. This in turn keeps that excellent soil structure in place that has taken so much work to achieve.

Garden Twine

There can be nothing more exciting than seeing a line of newly sown seeds germinating and nothing more disappointing than that line not being straight. Apart from the aesthetic pleasure gained from seeing a straight line, if a line of seedlings is not straight, it will either be taking up unnecessary space on one side or be too close to a row on the other. You can buy garden twine on a special holder, but winding the string onto two 18-inch (45-cm) lengths of bamboo is just as good.

When setting out your line, pull it tight and make sure that it is still tight when you are planting along its length and while making a shallow furrow. You need to check it on a regular basis to ensure that it has not moved. The simplest way to check it is to pull it upward, away from the soil, and let it go, and it will end up in the same position if it hasn't moved.

Knife

In the average garden, it is generally necessary to have only a pocket knife that can be used for a variety of jobs in the vegetable, herb, and fruit areas. A blunt knife is more dangerous than a sharp one, so be sure to keep your knife sharp by touching up the blade with a suitable sharpening stone on a regular basis.

Pruning Shears

In the fruit garden and herb areas, in particular, pruning shears will be used on a very regular basis, so a good-quality pair is a must. Not only will these last longer, but they will also produce a better cut and the better-quality blade will require less sharpening. There are two distinct types: anvil pruning shears or bypass pruning shears. The anvil types have the upper blade coming down onto a flat surface, whereas bypass pruning shears have the blade cutting past the usually curved lower section.

Some gardeners feel that the anvil types may bruise the branches and stems that are cut because the blade pushes them against the anvil in the process of cutting. With the bypass type, if the blade is not perfectly sharp, the stem or branch being cut will snag; in other words, it does not make a clean cut, leaving an uneven surface that will be more susceptible to disease. Pruning shears are akin to spades in gardeners' desire to tell you the best type, but as you can see they both have bad points in addition to their

Bypass-type pruning shears have curved blades.

being excellent cutting machines. On the plus side, some bypass pruning shears can be taken apart completely, which makes maintenance and blade sharpening very easy.

Pruning Saw

Used in the fruit garden, this piece of equipment is for cutting branches that are too large to be cut by pruning shears. A lot of pruning saws are now folding types, which makes them much safer to carry around, but, when making your purchase, ensure that the blade has a good locking system, so that when the blade is open it cannot suddenly shut onto your fingers.

Spade-Cleaning Tool

Plastic, wooden, and even metal models are available, but I have never bought one, preferring to make these very simple items myself. An odd piece of wood lying around can be cut into the correct shape and the edges then smoothed with a piece of sandpaper. It is worth keeping an edge on the flat cleaning end. This means that the tool does not really need to be too big, so 6 inches (15 cm) is generally long enough. It is a simple piece of equipment that is used to keep a spade blade clean of soil, making digging that much easier. As the soil begins to stick to the blade, the cleaning tool is run down the blade's length three or four times, before digging recommences.

Watering Can

A watering can is a must for any productive garden because it will direct water exactly where it is needed. Watering cans come in a range of shapes and sizes, as well as being made from plastic or metal, and in various colors. Always buy one that has a rose attachment. The most important point to remember is that you must be able to lift it high enough for watering when the watering can is completely full.

Rain Barrel

It is very important with the erratic weather patterns to have a rain barrel at the end of every available downspout to collect water for use on the productive areas. Make sure that the barrel is easily accessible and has an easy-to-use outlet point. Usually, you will need to stand the rain barrel on something, such as stacked bricks or something similar, so that you can access the outlet point. As water becomes scarce, the need for collecting our own becomes vital because vegetables and herbs will bolt very quickly if left to go dry, while fruit trees will start to drop their produce.

Hoses

Used correctly, hoses are not wasteful pieces of garden equipment, although it is essential to check before use whether there is a watering ban in place. In larger gardens, it is much easier to roll out a long hose and put the same amount of water onto your crops as would be done if traipsing backward and forward with a watering can. When buying a hose, look for a better-quality one that does not kink, and store it on a specially made reel, as it will then also last longer.

Rain barrels collect valuable water for use on your garden.

Soaker Hoses and Drip Irrigation

Soaker hoses or drip irrigation are essential for many short-term as well as long-term crops. You can lay a soaker hose on the ground next to the crop and attach it to a hose that runs to the water faucet. As long as the water is turned on, the hose will constantly drip water exactly where it is required. Soaker hoses are often made from recycled rubber, and the tiny openings in it allow water to easily seep out of the hose. Therefore, not much pressure is needed to force the water droplets out and into the soil. The great advantage of this is that it can be run from a rain barrel and does not need to be attached to a faucet. Drip irrigation is slightly different in that you can bury the pipe just under the ground next to the desired crop. I like to have a pipe running right next to each row of green beans.

Small holes allow the soaker hose to continually release droplets of water.

Pot Maker

The need to be more environmentally friendly is not going away, and recycling paper is one of the easiest things we can do. With a simple pot maker, you can use surplus newspaper by transforming it into small biodegradable pots that are ideal for starting seedlings. Then, when you are ready, you can transplant the seedlings directly, paper pots and all!

Firming Board

Firming boards are used for firming the soil when sowing into seed trays. You can buy them, but they are so easy to make. (See page 193 for instructions.)

Sprayer

Most organic gardeners will find a small hand sprayer sufficient, although some handheld pump-action types are worth considering for ease of use. You need only one sprayer—provided you clean it well after each use—because you will use it only for organically permissible insecticides or fungicides.

Chipper/Shredder

A chipper/shredder is an absolute must for the vegetable, herb, and fruit grower. All types of waste can be passed through a chipper/shredder and recycled into one part of the garden or the other. Tough vegetable and herb waste needs to be shredded before going onto the compost heap, while fruit bush and tree prunings can be shredded and then used as mulch. Do not be seduced by very cheap machines that will manage only to squash most of the material. With a chipper/shredder, you do definitely get what you pay for.

Lawn Mower

If you have grass paths on the vegetable plot or fruit trees growing in a grassed area, then a lawn mower is an essential piece of equipment for keeping this grass under control. I find that reel mowers work well at Barnsdale, although many different rotary mowers have rear rollers to leave lovely stripes after mowing. We do like to use a rotary mulching mower on certain areas; this chops the grass up so finely that it is not collected, but rather deposited back onto the ground to rot down. This piece of

A chipper/shredder is a big help in preparing materials for the compost heap.

The rapid action of the string chops weeds and long grass.

machinery is very much like the spade, in that all gardeners seem to have their own personal preference, for no other reason than they like and get along well with the mower they have.

String Trimmer

String trimmers (commonly known as "weed whackers") are used for tidying up around fruit trees and those areas that mowers cannot reach. It is important always to wear sturdy boots when using one of these, as well as a pair of goggles, to protect against the inevitable flying objects. The bulkier gas string trimmers will come with a string head, used for clearing long grass, weeds, and the like, and a blade head for tougher materials such as brambles. For gardeners who cannot cope with the weight of gas string trimmers, there is a range of excellent lightweight alternatives. It is also possible to buy a string trimmer with a revolving handle that will cut the lawn edges as well.

Seed Sowers

Many gardeners sow seed with their fairly nimble fingers. Unfortunately, this seed-sowing method, which is taken for granted by most, is not possible for all gardeners, so having a piece of equipment to do the job easily and fairly accurately is important for some. A ball sower uses the suction from a rubber ball to suck the seeds up a needle-like tube, so that they can then be released in the appropriate place. This is an excellent device for all seed sizes, as there are different sizes of tubes for the varying seed sizes.

For gardeners who do not have the use of their hands for sowing, there is also a mouth-operated seed sower available. It looks like a pen connected by a tube to the mouthpiece, and it is the suction created from the mouth that enables the seeds to be picked up and easily dropped on the surface of the soil. A filter is provided to prevent inhalation of any dust particles and seed.

Easy-Grip Add-On Handle
For gardeners with hand or wrist problems, this piece of equipment can make their work easier. It fits onto tools with handles up to 16 inches (40 cm) long. It is attached with a finger-operated wing nut and comes with an optional arm support.

Optional Equipment
Electric Tiller
An electric tiller, or rototiller, is a handy piece of machinery. Whether you own, borrow, or rent one, it will cultivate land and also prepare areas down to a fine tilth suitable

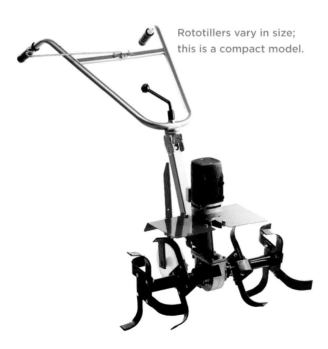

Rototillers vary in size; this is a compact model.

for direct seed sowing. They can be rear-wheel-driven or powered by the rotary blades at the front that churn the soil.

Electric tillers can be used regularly on light soils, but beware of using too often on heavy clay soils because the blades will smear the clay soil into an almost impenetrable barrier to water (called a pan), which will drastically impair drainage. Most modern machines will cultivate to a depth of between 6 and 9 inches (15 and 23 cm), so digging is required in most

years. On our clay soils, an electric mechanical cultivator is very useful, but we use it only if we haven't had enough time to dig the area manually.

Interchangeable Garden Tool Set
If space is limited for tool storage, or you have problems bending down, then an interchangeable garden tool set can be very helpful to you. These sets come in various sizes with varying handle lengths to suit gardeners of all heights. The vast range of tool heads available includes forks, trowels, rakes, hoes, tillers, edgers, rakes, loppers, shears, pruning saws, and more.

DIY Tools
Gardeners who prefer to make instead of buy garden structures (e.g., compost bins, hoophouses) will find equipment such as handsaws and screwdrivers very useful.

Sledgehammer/Club Hammer
Although you can dig holes and refill the soil around supporting stakes or fruit trees and soft fruit supports, I find that knocking them into the ground using a sledgehammer

or smaller club hammer will give a much firmer hold in the ground. Although these hammers are ideal for specific jobs, you might consider borrowing one because their general use in the productive garden is limited and may not warrant the purchase price.

Sprinkler

As with the hose, before you invest in a sprinkler, it is prudent to check whether it is possible to use one or whether they are covered under any water restrictions. Always look for sprinklers that are sturdy and have an adjustable sprinkler head that can be set to water only the areas requiring it. These types are able to water in a full circle or can be adjusted to water partial circles, ensuring that water is not wasted.

Lawn Edger

Although a spade can be used to keep the grass edges looking neat and tidy, the blade of a spade is slightly curved, so this straight-edged piece of equipment will do the job much better. For gardeners with back problems, longer-handled versions are available.

Edging Shears

Edging shears are another piece of equipment designed simply to keep the grass edges looking neat, so that they do not detract from the well-kept productive areas. Also available are lightweight shears, ones with longer or telescopic handles, and shears with geared blades, for gardeners with mobility problems. A wonderful addition to fit most edging shears is the edging-shears grass collector. This does exactly what it says it does by collecting the cut grass at the time of cutting. This saves on the job of having to collect it later.

Chapter 2

Preparing the Soil and Planting

The Soil

All crops will produce better if the ground they are to be sown or planted in is prepared to their specific requirements. This generally means a soil being of the correct structure and containing enough nutrients to sustain the crop for its harvesting life or the first season, if it is a long-term producer. The soil needs to be high in organic matter to obtain and maintain a good soil structure, and the most common way of getting this organic matter into the soil is to dig it in.

Digging

There are three basic manual methods of digging this organic matter into the soil and one using mechanical power. By far the most energetic but most rewarding method is double-digging, which is used to improve the soil to the deepest level by working organic matter down to a depth of about 16 inches (40 cm). If you are growing vegetables, it is important to obtain a good depth of topsoil so that the vegetables can grow nice, long, straight roots. Double-digging is not required on each plot every year, but in a four-year crop rotation one plot should be double-dug each year, then another one the next year, and so on. There is no benefit in double-digging each plot every year, as this would only create a soil that is too rich and cause problems such as forked roots on carrots and parsnips.

Single-digging uses the same principles as double-digging, only the manure is put at the bottom of the trench and not dug in. I like to single-dig two plots each year, and in my crop rotation plan I single-dig the two plots that follow the double-digging.

For the last plot in my crop rotation plan, I simply lightly mix the soil or use an electric tiller. This plot is the one that I reserve for root crops; because they require minimal fertilization and organic matter, there is no need to go to the lengths of digging. I like to lightly turn the soil using a garden fork, breaking up any clumps of soil as I go to create the perfect seedbed.

Mechanical cultivation uses a rototiller or cultivator to break up and prepare the soil. This is by far the easiest of the cultivation methods, but it does have its pitfalls. You run the machine over the soil after you've placed a generous layer of well-rotted manure or compost on the surface, turning it into the soil. You can also use either of these machines to break up uneven soil to create the perfect fine tilth for a seedbed. You can use an electric tiller frequently on light and sandy soils, although it will not get the organic matter down to the depths achieved by single-digging.

On heavier or clay soils, the spinning blades of an electric tiller can smear the soil, creating a pan that prevents the passage of water through the soil, which can then lead to waterlogging problems. The pan also causes problems with root crops because it is difficult for them to grow through it, and their roots will fork.

How to Double-Dig a Plot

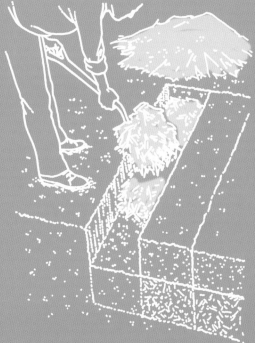

First, dig out a trench about 4 feet (120 cm) wide, 12 inches (30 cm) across, and 8 inches (20 cm) deep; either pile the dug-out soil next to the trench or put it in a wheelbarrow. If you are digging a larger plot, then dig up and down so that you can incorporate the soil taken out of the first trench into the trench at the end of the row on the way back. If you are digging only one stretch, you will have to put the soil into a wheelbarrow and drop it at the end of the area to be dug. Next, put plenty of well-rotted manure into the bottom of the trench and then dig it into the subsoil, going down about 8 inches (20 cm). Once you've done this, dig out a trench of identical proportions directly behind the first one and throw the soil into the empty first trench, adding plenty of organic matter as you do this.

No-Dig Method

It is funny how a gardener's eyes light up when you talk to him or her about a method of growing vegetables and herbs that requires no digging. It is not, however, the be-all-and-end-all, and it's certainly no reason to sell your spade!

When growing vegetables or herbs using the no-dig system, I have always found it best to double-dig the area first—this gives a better starting platform and a shorter wait for good crops. After this initial exertion, you will not have to do any further digging because this system relies on a healthy population of soil organisms to do the work instead. You add organic matter to the soil as a mulch and then leave it to the worms, beetles, and other creepy crawlies to take this organic mulch into the soil. You can lightly rake this organic matter into the soil surface.

Most crops are grown in the same way as with a conventionally dug soil. One exception is potatoes, where they can be placed onto the soil surface and covered with straw or black plastic, so that the light is eliminated. If you grow potatoes under black plastic, you will need to cut small slits in the plastic as the potato tops push it up. This allows the tops to grow through, while the tubers form in the dark beneath the plastic. If you use straw on the soil surface, make sure you use plenty so that light is not allowed through. The potato tops generally push their way through the straw, although occasionally they may need a bit of directing.

The advantages of this system, in addition to the obvious saving of personal energy, is that weed growth is generally less, as the mulch prevents growth and the lack of cultivation does not encourage weed seeds to germinate. The lack of cultivation and mulch also conserves water in the soil, easing the initial water requirements of crops.

The no-dig system is ideal for those people who have back or mobility problems, and is excellent for use in conjunction with the bed system.

Preparing a Seedbed

It is worth spending the time in preparing the soil so that seeds germinate well, to maximize the potential of all crops. If you have a heavy or clay soil, it is a good idea first to cover the area required for sowing with a piece of plastic. This prevents the soil from becoming too wet to work, while also warming it up to give those early crops a head start. As a lot of vegetable seeds are quite small, they are unable to push through large clods of soil or a capped soil surface. This means that the most important part of preparing a seedbed is to ensure a fine tilth at the end. First, the soil needs to be tilled. If it is part of a crop rotation, then there is no need to add any extra organic matter.

Be sure to use enough straw that the thickness eliminates the light.

Once the soil has been dug and the larger clods broken up with a fork, the whole area needs to be raked to leave a level area consisting of fine soil particles. For most crops, I add pelleted chicken manure prior to raking; this provides ample food for the growing crop. If it is still too early to sow seeds into the soil, then cover the area with plastic.

Stale Seedbed Method

This is a very useful technique if the next crop to be sown is a slow-maturing type, such as parsnips, where the annual weeds will grow more rapidly than the crop, smothering it before it has a chance to mature. If you are plagued with annual weeds, the stale seedbed method can also be used to help resolve the problem before any crop is planted.

There are two basic methods that can be employed to obtain the same end result. The first is to prepare the area to be sown about three to four weeks before it is required, then leave it so that the annual weeds can grow. As soon as there is a good flush of weeds, use a hoe to cut off the tops and put these tops on the compost heap. As they have not had a chance to flower and seed, this should greatly reduce any further germination of annual weeds, allowing the crop to germinate and grow without unwanted competition. The second method is to cover the ground with a sheet of black plastic about six to eight weeks before use. The soil underneath will be heated, encouraging the weeds to grow, and they will subsequently die due to the lack of light. I tend to use this method more in the early part of the growing season, as the plastic also warms the ground in anticipation of the crop when it is sown, and the crop therefore gets a really good start. As the season progresses and the weather improves, the benefit of warming the soil for the crop diminishes.

Organic Matter

Organic matter is very important in producing a well-structured and naturally fertile soil. Before soil was actively cultivated to produce food, the organic matter that went into it came from vegetation that was naturally shed, such as leaves, and any animals that died. These would rot down and be taken into the soil by organisms and insects, which is how topsoil was created, long before it was bagged and sold in the garden center. It is the organic matter that is the vital constituent of soil when creating a good structure. Organic matter enables good drainage in heavy soils, conserves moisture in lighter soils, and produces a perfect environment for roots to grow. There are several different types of organic matter that can be added to the soil.

Garden Compost

Garden compost is the most common organic matter put into the soil, as it is the easiest to come by, generally being produced on site. The great thing about it is that the quality of the final product is controllable. If you manage the compost heap correctly, the nutrient levels should be balanced and the finished compost almost like loam. Good-quality garden compost adds bulk to the soil, improves

You can produce garden compost easily, creating a nutrient-rich soil amendment.

drainage where required, and conserves moisture on lighter soils. It also adds vital nutrients to the soil. I aim to produce three lots of compost from my bin each year: two during the spring, summer, and autumn, and one through the winter. By putting material into the bin in thin layers and turning the compost once a month, I can convert raw compostable material to friable compost in three months during the warmer weather, and six months in winter. The most important factor to take into consideration when choosing garden compost, however, is that it is free.

Farmyard Manure

Farmyard manure includes cow and horse manure that has been well rotted before incorporating. It adds the same things to the soil as compost. The main problems with any farmyard manure are that it is much harder to come by if you live in the city than if you live in the country and it can upset close neighbors because of the inevitable smell. An overriding problem for the organic gardener, however, is to ensure that any farmyard manure is obtained from a clean farm. The cleaner and more well kept the farm, the less likelihood the manure will be infected with weed seeds.

Leaves make excellent compost but take a long time to break down.

Leaf Mold

Leaf mold is another free commodity, depending on how many trees you have in your garden or whether you live close to a park or public woods. Leaves make an excellent soil conditioner, but they can take between one and three years to break down, depending on the types of leaves. It is the amount of lignin contained in leaves that dictates how long decomposition will take, as some leaves have much more of this fibrous tissue than others. Although leaf mold makes an excellent soil conditioner, the experience of having to wait three years for our beech leaves to rot down means I much prefer to use the result as a seed or potting soil, as it has an excellent structure and consistent nutrient levels.

Kitchen Compost

Kitchen compost (sometimes called green compost) is an end product of recycling the green trash we discard. The recycling plant removes all of the materials that will not biodegrade quickly, with the remainder being composted in big heaps. Once ready, it is bagged and sold back to us at a greatly inflated price. Due to the complete lack of control over what is discarded and the amounts of each item included, the end result is

Cleaning Weedy Ground

If you have moved onto a property where the garden has been neglected and is a weedy mess, the best way to get this type of ground under control and clean for growing vegetables, herbs, and fruit is to grow vegetables—more precisely, potatoes. This crop is an excellent ground "cleaner" due to the amount of soil cultivation the crop requires before and during the time the crop is in the ground, as well as the soil coverage of the potato tops (stems).

You will need to clear the ground of weeds by digging out the perennial weeds and hoeing off the annual ones. Once the weed tops have been cleared, the soil can be prepared by digging and adding organic matter. The potatoes are then planted into furrows or planted using a trowel. Once they are planted, it is a good idea to grow a quick catch crop (see page 14) between the rows, such as radish, scallion, or lettuce transplanted from seed trays (flats) with individual cells. Once these crops have been harvested, the potato tops will require earthing up. This is the process of drawing up soil from between the rows of potatoes so that the new tops are almost completely covered with soil. This will keep the developing potatoes covered with soil and not exposed to any light. If the potatoes do push out of the ground into the light, they will turn green and become inedible.

It may be necessary to earth up, or hill, the potato tops three times. As the tops fill out, they cover the ground, excluding light, making the conditions beneath this foliage unattractive to growing weeds. It is also wise to sheet-mulch between the rows, which will not only conserve vital moisture for the crop but also prevent weed growth. Virtually at the end of the growing season, the soil is again cultivated to harvest the main-crop potatoes, clearing any weeds that may have grown. It is then too late for weeds to germinate and grow successfully before the winter sets in. This is a wonderful organic method for clearing ground, with the added bonus of food at the end of it!

You can make your own kitchen compost for free instead of purchasing it.

a compost that can have very variable nutrient levels, which makes it suitable only as a soil conditioner.

Spent Mushroom Compost

This is really well-rotted horse manure that has had the pH level raised to make it alkaline, a condition that is favored by mushrooms. Be aware of the pH of your soil before you use spent mushroom compost, as too much may raise the pH to a level beyond what your crops prefer.

Seaweed

Seaweed is an excellent and free soil conditioner if you live by the coast. As it rots down very quickly, seaweed can be added raw to the soil and dug in. Although the nutrient levels may be variable, it does contain vital trace elements, but I would be wary of seaweed taken from areas of poor-quality seawater.

Peat

Peat has little or no nutrients in it, so is incorporated into the soil only to add bulk. There are better, cheaper, and more environmentally sustainable alternatives.

Green Manures

Green manures are grown in productive areas when the ground is empty between crops. They are very good for the soil, as everything will be dug into the soil, adding vital bulk, with some also fixing nitrogen on their roots (see sidebar on pages 44–45).

Sheep Manure

Sheep manure makes an excellent liquid feed as well as adding nutrients to the soil if incorporated. Sheep are naturally roaming animals, however, so collecting the manure is a backbreaking and laborious task using a hand and bucket.

Chicken Manure

Chicken manure is much easier to collect than sheep manure. Confining hens to henhouses at night produces a lot of manure. Use only manure collected from the henhouses of free-range chickens and ensure that it is well composted; otherwise, it will have far too high a nutrient level and burn off your crops.

Pig Manure

This is an excellent manure due to the high nutrient content, but it is important to ensure that the manure comes from organic farms to avoid any unwanted chemicals leaching into your soil.

Manure from free-range chickens makes an excellent fertilizer.

Green Manures

There are many different types of green manure, each performing a vital role in maintaining an excellent soil structure and composition. Their great asset is that they never take up valuable space, as they are always used on land that is vacant or between crops; in this respect, a green manure can only benefit the soil. There are two distinct types of green manure: nitrogen fixers and non-nitrogen fixers. The former will fix nitrogen in nodules on their roots in a form that is much more readily available to the crops that will be grown in that soil. Some of these nitrogen fixers will have very long taproots and thus are ideal if you are using the no-dig method of gardening.

If the nitrogen attached to the roots of the first group of green manures is so beneficial to the soil, why grow non-nitrogen fixers? This is a very good question and one that is easily answered. Non-nitrogen-fixing green manures tend to be very quick, whereas the nitrogen fixers are longer-term manures. Therefore, non-nitrogen-fixing green manures can be used in areas that will have a reasonably quick turnaround in crops. Although they do not add nitrogen, they do add organic bulk to the soil.

Nitrogen Fixers

ALFALFA (*Medicago sativa*)—Alfalfa is a deep-rooted type that can be sown at a rate of $^1/_2$ ounce/square yard (15 g/sq m). Sow in spring and dig in during autumn, or sow late summer and dig in during spring.

FAVA (BROAD) BEAN (*Vicia fabia*) —Use a field bean or a winter-hardy variety, such as 'Aquadulce Claudia.' Sow 4 inches (10 cm) apart in the autumn or early summer, in rows 12 inches (30 cm) apart. It is also possible to harvest some of the beans, but do not let the plants become too woody before digging under; otherwise, they will decompose much more slowly.

RED CLOVER (*Trifolium pratense*)—Sow in spring or late summer, and always before autumn, at a rate of 1 ounce/square yard (30 g/sq m). Leave to grow and dig in when the land is required for the next crop.

LUPIN (*Lupinus angustifolius*)—Lupins are rapid growers that will become very woody if left too long. In spring, sow 3 inches (8 cm) apart in rows 6 inches (15 cm) apart. Cut down and dig in during summer or when the shoots become firm but not woody. As well as adding nitrogen to the soil, lupins also add phosphates.

WINTER VETCH (*Vicia villosa*)—Winter vetch is helpful because it grows in milder climates during winter when land is vacant. In late summer, sow 3 inches (8 cm) apart in rows 6 inches (15 cm) apart; dig in during spring.

Non-nitrogen Fixers

RYE (*Secale cereale*)—The extensive root system of this type of green manure aids with soil structure while the plentiful green matter produced above ground adds much-needed bulk to a soil. Sow in late summer or early autumn at a rate of 1 ounce/square yard (30 g/sq m) and dig in during spring.

PHACELIA (*Phacelia tanacelifolia*)—Phacelia is one of the best green manures, as it is fast growing and adds plenty of bulk to the soil. It is important to dig it in when it is still soft, so that it does not rob the soil of any nitrogen. As it is not hardy, sow after frosts have finished in spring or early summer, at a rate of 1 ounce/4 square yards (30 g/ 4 sq m), and dig in eight weeks after sowing.

WHITE MUSTARD (*Sinapsis alba*)—White mustard is a very rapid grower that can be sown any time after the last frost until the frosts begin again in the autumn. Dig in before flowering, usually after about four weeks. Sow at a rate of 1 ounce/4 square yards (30 g/ 4 sq m). The one drawback of this manure is that, being a member of the cabbage family, it could harbor clubroot.

ITALIAN RYEGRASS (*Lolium multiflorum*)—Use the 'Westerwolds' variety of ryegrass because it will not cause problems with regrowth, unlike the perennial or biennial varieties. It adds plenty of bulk to the soil and is tolerant of colder soils, so it can be sown before more tender crops such as summer squash or beans are planted. The other advantage of Italian ryegrass is that it is a rapid germinator that can be sown at a rate of 1 ounce/4 square yards (30 g/ 4 sq m) between quick turnaround crops.

Once the green manure has reached the end of its time, whether because it is coming up to seed or because the ground is ready for the next productive crop, it must be wilted before digging into the ground. Not only will it decompose in the ground much quicker if it is wilted before digging in, but wilting will also prevent regrowth, which can be a problem, particularly with ryegrass.

To wilt the green manure, cut off the tops at ground level either with a hoe or by chopping at soil level with a spade. Leave the tops on the soil surface for a couple of days and then dig them under once they are thoroughly wilted. As you can see from the list of nitrogen fixers, the legumes (peas and beans) fix nitrogen on their roots. When you've finished harvesting one of these crops and are ready to remove the plants, always chop off the tops at ground level and leave the roots in the ground so that the plants that follow in that space can benefit from that available nitrogen.

The benefits of both types of green manure are that they both add bulk to the soil and cover it, therefore reducing water loss and preventing weed growth. I have also used mustard as a quick crop to draw water out of a very wet piece of ground prior to the next crop being sown.

Starting and Propagating Plants

P ropagation is where it all starts. With vegetables and herbs, the plants will be started into growth by one of four methods. Fruit trees are a slightly different matter because most trees are bought either as one-year-old single-stemmed plants, known as "whips," or as partially trained trees. Soft fruit can also be propagated to bulk up stocks or simply to replace old and unproductive plants. Each method of propagation is covered in great detail, so that successful initial production of crops should be a mere formality.

Sowing Seeds

This is the most commonly used method of propagation for vegetables and many herbs, as it is cheap and, in most cases, very successful. The primary consideration before sowing seed is whether the seed is viable. It is not always cost-effective to use fresh seed each year, as some seed packets contain enough seed to keep a family supplied in that particular vegetable for several years. The seeds usually come in a paper outer packet. In some cases, the seeds are sealed in a foil packet inside. In most cases, this foil packet will keep the seeds fresh for more than one season. By the end of the growing season, you may have seeds such as radish, lettuce, carrots, any of the brassicas, leeks, and so on left over. If so, fold the end of the foil packet to reseal the seeds inside, place the packet back into its original paper packet (so that you know what the seeds are), and put it away in a cool place until required the following year. I keep seed for only one extra year before discarding it, as germination becomes less reliable. The most unreliable vegetable variety from seed is undoubtedly parsnips, with the seed only being viable if it is fresh, so these cannot be kept for more than the season in which they were bought.

Cardboard egg cartons work well for chitting potatoes.

Apart from correctly sowing the seed, the most important job is to label everything—otherwise, things can get very confusing. I like to put as much information on the label as I can, with the plant type and variety on one side and the date sown and a code for the seed company marked on the reverse. It may never be used, but I find it useful to follow the crop from sowing date to harvest for future reference. Also, as far as the seed company is concerned, if there is poor germination one year with seeds from the same company, it is worthwhile information to have.

Seed Preparation

Some seed requires special treatment before it can be sown. Two good examples of this are parsley and potatoes. Parsley germinates at a much faster rate and more evenly if it is treated with boiling water first. The boiling will break the built-in dormancy of the seed, allowing it to germinate in two to three days. The seeds can be put into a dish, the water poured onto them, drained, and the seeds left to dry before sowing, or they can be sown and the water very carefully poured over them in situ. The problem with the second method is that if too much water is poured too quickly, most of the seed will be washed to the outer extremities of the seed tray.

Although called seed potatoes, they are not strictly seed; however, potatoes perform much better if "chitted" before sowing. To chit the potatoes, place them on a tray with individual compartments (an egg carton works well to hold the potatoes in place); for each potato, the end with the most eyes should point upward. Place your tray(s) in a light, warm place to initiate growth, for example, under greenhouse benches. Small shoots will begin to grow out from the eyes, at which point you can plant the potatoes. This method of starting their growth before planting means that, after planting, the potatoes will just keep growing and give a more rapid return than if planted without chitting.

Sowing into Seed Trays

Sowing into seed trays means that crops can be started earlier and raised in a greenhouse, under a cold frame, or on a windowsill before they are sown directly into the ground at the appropriate time. Regardless what size seed tray you are using, the sowing method is the same.

Before you start, ensure that the seed tray is clean; if it has been used previously, pests and diseases can be carried from crop to crop on soil or plant debris. First, overfill the seed tray with soil—make sure that there are no lumps by rubbing the soil between your hands as you fill. Next, slightly lift each end of the seed tray and drop back down two or three times to settle the soil into the tray. Using a firming board (see page 193), level the soil off at the top of the tray and then press the firming board down onto the soil gently, just enough to compress it a little.

Always water the soil well with a watering can and rose before sowing, as this prevents the seed from being washed to the sides of the tray, as it would be if you watered after sowing. The seed can then be sown thinly and evenly across the surface of the soil.

I find it much easier to sow the seed from the slightly cupped palm of my hand. This cupping makes a nice groove right in the center of the hand and, when I tap my hand gently, the seed is channeled at an even pace down the groove and onto the soil surface, giving a nice, even seed spacing. It is far easier to control seed using this method than sowing directly from the packet or sowing by gently letting seed fall from between your finger and thumb. The seed can then be covered with a thin layer of vermiculite.

Using a small pot to do this job works very well. I find vermiculite better than other products and soil because it allows light to reach the seed, eventually breaks down in the soil, and does not form a hard crust on the surface, as peat does. The seed tray can then be put into a propagator with artificial heat, or simply set on greenhouse benches, under a cold frame, or on a windowsill until the seed germinates. The unheated seeds will germinate, albeit more slowly than the artificially heated ones.

Sowing into Plug Trays

This is a different procedure than sowing into seed trays because it involves sowing into many individual cells that collectively make up the plug tray. When propagating vegetables or herbs, I usually use trays with at least fifty-four cells, but no smaller; otherwise, the plants will begin to starve before they are big enough to plant. As with seed trays, overfill the plug tray with soil, tap each end to consolidate the soil, and level off any excess at the top using your hand. Next, make a small indentation in the soil in each cell for the seeds to be dropped into, leaving enough room to cover the seeds with vermiculite. Once you've prepared every cell, you can sow the seeds into these indentations, aiming to place one to three seeds in each cell.

After the seeds have germinated and the seedlings have reached the first true leaf stage, you'll remove the weaker seedlings to leave one seedling per cell. A key aspect

Sow one to three seeds into the indentations you've made in each cell.

of growing in plug trays is that you can repot or plant the plugs (the mini plants) directly from the plug tray without the need for transplanting. This eliminates the potential for root damage and therefore keeps the young plants growing at their maximum rate.

Sowing in plug trays is not suitable for all vegetables and herbs. This system is used primarily for varieties that germinate readily because a lot of space and soil is taken up if the seeds fail. It is also possible to transplant seedlings from a seed tray into plug trays to avoid wasting soil. These plants would then be planted directly from the plug tray.

With vegetables such as leeks, onions, carrots, beets (beetroot), kohlrabi, and turnips, you can use these plugs for the multi-sowing method. This is an excellent way of producing young, tender, and quick crops in limited space and thus is ideally suited to the bed system. You fill the tray and make indentations in the same manner as previously described, but you drop between five and seven seeds into each cell and do not thin the seedlings. You then plant the plugs in their little clumps, and, as they mature, each one will push the others out of its way.

With beets (beetroot), for example, you harvest the roots when they reach golf-ball size; you can either pull them individually, harvest them as needed, or harvest the whole clump at one time. With the latter, you can get a crop of young and tender beets in a very short time that is equivalent to each root of the much slower-to-mature individual roots of main-crop beets.

Sowing into Pots and Tubes

The two previous sowing methods are perfectly adequate for smaller seeds, but the larger types need larger containers. Seeds of melons, cucumbers, zucchini (courgettes), summer squash (marrows), and some companion plants are better sown into 3-inch (8-cm) pots or tubes. You can purchase pots made from various materials or make them yourself, while the tubes are generally either made of "whalehide" (cardboard coated in bitumen) or homemade from several sheets of recycled newspaper. Newspaper is fine to use in an organic garden as long as it has only black print, and it makes very cheap pots and tubes. Overfill the pot or tube with soil, tap on the potting bench, and level off the soil. You can then push the seed into the soil and water the whole thing. You can plant compressed coir pots, newspaper, and whalehide as complete units, and they will break down in the soil.

Sowing onto Tissue Paper and into Jars

Sowing onto tissue paper and into jars probably gives you the easiest and quickest return of all sowing methods. The seeds of both mustard and cress will germinate on moist tissue paper placed in the bottom of a seed tray. It is important to keep the tissue paper moist; these seeds germinate perfectly happily in less than a week, either in the greenhouse or on a windowsill. Mung beans are very nutritious and can be grown in either a jar or a bowl. They need to be soaked for about twelve hours, drained, and then put into their growing containers in a warm room, but not in direct sunlight. Fill the jar with water every day and drain to rinse the beans. Depending on how much root you want on your beans, they can be harvested from as little as two days after their initial soaking, up to about a week.

Sowing into a Gutter

This simple technique is used primarily for peas but can also be used with other crops. It is an excellent way to start peas off early that takes up little or no space in the greenhouse. I also use this method instead of sowing straight outside because of problems with mice removing and eating all the directly sown seeds. A length of gutter is filled with soil and leveled off. I use two pots at each end of the gutter to stop the soil from falling out.

The seeds are sown in succession, with the next length of gutter sown once the seedlings in the first reach a height of 2 inches (5 cm). They can be hardened off and then transplanted once the plants have reached 3 inches (8 cm) high. When they are ready to be planted, you make a furrow with a hoe, place one end of the gutter in the far end of the furrow, and then, as you move the gutter backward, the rooted peas will slide effortlessly into the prepared furrow.

Pregerminating Seed

Pregerminating is a widely used and simple technique for parsnip seeds, as they are notoriously poor germinators. Pregerminating the seed eliminates the problems associated with erratic germination where a row will contain parts that have a seedling every 1 inch (2½ cm) and then 24–36 inches (60–90 cm) with no seedlings germinated at all. As parsnips also move very poorly, it is not feasible to lift seedlings and replant

Germinating seed before sowing encourages consistency in the crop.

in the gaps. Getting the seed started inside first provides the opportunity to see which seed is viable and will continue to grow. The part-germinated seed can then be sown at their required spacing for a really even crop. Place the seed onto a piece of moist tissue paper (which must be kept moist while waiting for the seed to begin germinating). It is better if the seeds are given a bit of gentle heat, as this will help to get an even germination. You do not want to leave the seeds to germinate too far, as inevitable damage will be caused when they are handled during sowing.

Handle seedlings gently when transplanting, not by the stems, as shown here.

Transplanting Seedlings

Once you've sown your seeds into trays and they have germinated and produced their first true leaves, the seedlings are large enough to handle and are ready to be transplanted. This is the process of moving the seedlings from the seed tray either into cells or small pots so that they can continue to grow. It is a delicate process because the seedlings can be damaged very easily at this stage, and seedlings with little to no root damage will grow much faster than damaged ones. The principle is to remove the seedling from the soil in the seed tray, causing as little damage to the roots as possible, transferring it to a larger container. It is possible to buy special tools for teasing out the seedlings from the soil, but I find a short piece of cane or a pencil does the job more than adequately. Hold the seedling by the old seed leaves and gently ease the roots out of the soil. Once the seed tray is empty, the soil can go straight onto the compost heap.

Transplanting Plants and Trees

Transplanting is the process of putting plants and trees into the ground when not raised in their final position. Pot- and cell-raised vegetable and herb plants need to be transplanted into the ground with the top of the soil of their original container buried just below soil level. Soil-raised vegetables (such as brassicas), divided herbs, and fruit trees all need to have the new soil level at the same height as it was in their previous position. Burying vegetables, herbs, and fruit too deeply can cause them to rot, while not transplanting deeply enough can cause plants and trees to dry out.

Hardening Off

Hardening off is a vital procedure for all plants that have been started inside. If a plant is removed from a very warm environment and placed into a much more exposed and colder one, it is plain to see that its growth rate could stop or slow down dramatically. Plants raised inside therefore need to be acclimatized to the outside conditions gradually. For greenhouse-raised plants, this means moving them into a cold frame or tunnel for a few days before planting; those raised in a cold frame need to be well ventilated prior to planting for a similar effect.

Direct Sowing

The most commonly used method is to sow in situ. It involves no expensive materials but it is limited by climatic conditions, as most vegetable varieties can be sown outside only once the temperatures have increased for germination and to ensure the soft seedling tops are not burnt off by severe frosts. Smaller seeds are planted into narrow furrows that are created using the corner of a hoe or rake or a bit of cane.

Each vegetable or herb variety will have a depth at which it needs to be sown—usually between ½ and 1 inch (1 and 2½ cm) deep. It is important to water the bottom of the furrow at this stage to avoid watering overhead initially; watering first prevents the soil surface from "capping" (becoming crusty and almost impenetrable to the germinating seed) while still giving the seed the moisture it requires for germination. The seed is then thinly and evenly sown down the length of the furrow.

Potatoes, directly sown in a shallow furrow.

The soil on the edges of the furrow is pulled back over the seed and gently firmed. I always label each end of the row so that if one is lost or pulled out by birds, I still have a record of what was sown.

Fluid Sowing

Fluid sowing is a method that can be used with seeds that have been pregerminated, and it is one that is not restricted to parsnips—you can use it on any crop that requires thinning. This system can be used for most smaller-seeded vegetable varieties and will give an even sowing of seeds that yields an earlier crop because the seeds will grow much quicker. Once the radicle (small root) is seen on most of the seeds, it is time to sow.

You can buy a special kit, but I like to use a clear plastic freezer bag and fungicide-free wallpaper paste because they are much cheaper and just as effective. The

Brassica Seedbed

Because all brassicas move very well, it is more economic to grow them into the seedling stage and then transplant them into their final positions. For a faster crop, it is advisable to sow them into a cold frame. The idea is to sow the amount required thinly but evenly into short furrows inside the cold frame and then leave them to germinate. Once they reach a height of 3 inches (8 cm), the seedlings should be touching each other in one continuous row. They can then be lifted and carefully separated.

Brassicas can suffer a check in growth from lack of water soon after transplanting. To give them the best start possible, place them into a small water-filled trench once lifted from the seedbed. They can be left there for a couple of hours while they take up any water they require; as an added bonus, their roots will be covered with a film of wet soil that aids establishment. They will still require a good watering after transplanting.

wallpaper paste is mixed and the seeds stirred into it so that they are well dispersed. The seeded paste is then poured into the plastic bag. Once a furrow has been prepared outside, one corner of the bag is cut and the paste is squeezed out along the length of the furrow. It is rather like squeezing icing out of an icing bag onto a cake.

Once the line of paste has been dispensed, the furrow is refilled with soil and watered. Do not let the soil dry out for the first few days, as this may cause the paste to harden and therefore not allow the seed to grow out of it.

Station Sowing

Station sowing is a technique used with pregerminated seed or for varieties that do not germinate well, such as parsnip. If using pregerminated seed, place it at the final spacing for the crop so that no thinning is required—the seed is 99.9 percent certain to keep growing. This method is used with crops that germinate poorly to ensure a good, even spacing of the crop. Make a furrow, as for direct sowing, and sow two or three seeds at the final crop spacing and cover them as usual. The likelihood is that at least one seed will germinate at each station, giving a perfectly spaced crop. If more than one seed germinates, thin the weaker plants, leaving the strongest to grow.

Thinning

There are not many gardeners that either have a precision sowing machine or have mastered the art of sowing by hand to such a degree that they can be absolutely precise. Therefore, most vegetable varieties sown directly into the ground will need to be thinned at some stage. The thinning process involves leaving the crop until the seedlings are of a manageable size but not too big. Any unwanted seedlings are generally pulled out by hand.

Most pulled-out seedlings cannot be used for anything and will wilt very quickly, so they generally end up on the compost heap. Some crops, however, are thinned at a point where the thinnings can be used. With beets (beetroot), radishes, mini vegetables, parsnips, kohlrabi, Florence fennel, scallions, and early carrot varieties, the whole crop is left in situ and the larger plants pulled as soon as they are of a size where they are useful. This continues as the crop matures and will ultimately leave enough space for the remainder of the plants to grow on into a useful size.

Thinning a crop means removing seedlings by hand.

Cuttings

The primary form of propagation for herbs, some soft fruits, and the occasional vegetable is through cuttings. There are four methods, with each variety usually suited to one particular method.

Softwood Cuttings

Softwood cuttings give the quickest return, but they are also the ones most likely to fail—once taken as cuttings, these soft shoots are less stable than other types of cuttings and are prone to disease and rapid loss of water. They are usually taken when the plant is growing at its strongest and producing plenty of soft and sap-filled growing tips and side shoots. It is these healthy, soft shoots that are required, and tips of between 2 and 4 inches (5 and 10 cm) are removed, just above a pair of leaves, with a pair of sharp pruning shears, a knife, or a pair of scissors. The cuttings are then put straight into a plastic bag to minimize any water loss and increase their chances of rooting successfully. The length of stem at the base of the cutting is then removed just below the bottom set of leaves with a clean horizontal cut. As the cutting is going to be pushed into soil, it is important to remove carefully half to three-quarters of the bottom leaves, as they are not required.

The cuttings can then be inserted into a 3-inch (8-cm) pot, with three to five cuttings per pot. Push the bare stem right into the soil and water well. A plastic bag is then fixed over the pot and the cuttings to retain moisture.

The plastic bag ensures constant moisture is kept around the leaves of the cuttings, reducing water loss and therefore preventing the cutting from wilting. In the summer, in a cold greenhouse, or on a windowsill, the cuttings should root within about four weeks, at which point they can be gently teased apart and potted individually into 3-inch (8-cm) pots. If you have a propagator, the cuttings can be put into this to root; if the propagator is set at a temperature of 70°F (21°C), rooting time can be cut in half. This is an ideal method for increasing stocks of most herb species, such as *Thymus* (thyme), *Oregano* (marjoram), *Rosmarinus* (rosemary), *Mentha* (mint), *Lavandula* (lavender), and many others.

Semiripe Cuttings

Semiripe cuttings are taken in exactly the same way as softwood cuttings and can be inserted into soil or directly into the ground, inside a cold frame. They are called "semiripe" because the cuttings are taken later, usually from July onward, from growth that is a little older and not so soft. This means that they have therefore ripened more. They are usually longer than softwood cuttings and need to be 4–6 inches (10–15 cm) long. Look for a shoot that is growing at the top but riper at the base, and cut just below a leaf joint as before. Remove about half of the bottom leaves, close to the stem, and insert into either compost or prepared and improved soil in a cold frame. I like to mix the soil in the cold frame with equal parts soil, compost, and coarse grit or gravel to a depth of 4 inches (10 cm), as this makes the perfect rooting medium.

If the potential cuttings are a bit short, it is possible to employ another method that will obtain the required amount of ripened growth, and that is to take a heel cutting. Removing it from the plant is easy because you don't need pruning shears. You simply hold the shoot firmly and pull it sharply away from the plant so that part of the stem

Hardwood cuttings are the most stable, and thus easiest, type of cuttings to propogate.

comes away with it. This part of the stem is called a "heel," and you can trim it flush with the cutting stem before inserting it into the soil or ground.

Because they are older and riper, semiripe cuttings do not contain as much sap-filled new growth, and so are more stable than softwood cuttings and less liable to fail. Rooting will take longer, but once it has taken place the cuttings can be lifted and repotted as before. This method can be used to propagate blueberries.

Hardwood Cuttings

Hardwood cuttings are the easiest and cheapest method of propagation, as the cuttings are the most stable, due to the time of year they are taken, and there is minimal water loss and less risk of disease than with the previous two methods. The time to take these cuttings is in the autumn or early winter, once all the leaves have fallen. You are looking for a cutting that is of pencil width and about 8 inches (20 cm) long—luckily, just the length of a pair of pruning shears.

Look for a healthy bud, and just below this bud cut horizontally across the stem. From this horizontal cut, move about 8 inches (20 cm) up the shoot to another healthy bud and cut above it, with a slanting cut, so that the top of the cut is above the bud. Ensure that the bottom of the cut is not below the bottom of the bud. If it does come below the bottom of this top bud, it will cut off the bud's water and food supply, causing first the bud, then the shoot, to die back to the next healthy bud. The slanting cut allows rainwater to run off the top of the bud, minimizing rotting problems as well as giving an excellent platform for your thumb to sit on when you are pushing the cuttings into the soil.

Push the cuttings into a cultivated piece of ground, leaving a third of the top showing above the soil. If setting the cuttings in straight lines, don't forget to use a garden line to ensure the straightest of rows. Firm in and leave for a year to root. Keep watered throughout the growing season and, in the early winter, lift and plant in their permanent positions. This is the best method for propagating black currants, red currants, white currants, and gooseberries.

Root Cuttings

Root cuttings are a good way to propagate sea kale. This perennial vegetable is an excellent source of stems, leaves, and flower heads in the spring, which can be eaten raw or cooked. In October or November, either completely dig up a sea kale plant or gently dig around it so that the roots can be accessed. Remove enough root for the amount of cuttings required. They can be cut into 3- to 6-inch (8- to 15-cm) sections, with a flat cut denoting the top of the root and a sloping cut at the bottom.

The root cuttings are then placed into a large enough pot or a cold frame filled with soil or coarse sand, so that they are just covered. In the spring, they should begin to shoot from the tops, when they can be lifted and planted. Prior to planting, ensure that all buds except for the strongest one are rubbed off the root cutting. The strong bud is left to grow into a new sea kale plant.

Division

Division is a simple method used for some herbs and soft fruit. Once the plants have become dormant, anytime from the end of October until early March, they can be lifted and split up into smaller pieces, before being replanted. They can be split using your hands, if it is only a small clump. For larger clumps, push two forks into the clump back to back and then lever so that the clump splits.

This splitting and putting back of smaller pieces revitalizes the clumps so that they produce more fruit. It will also have the added bonus of providing leftover plantlets that can be used elsewhere in the garden or given away to friends and family.

Strawberry plants produce long, flexible stems, or *runners*, that grow their own roots and can be cut and planted separately.

Layering

Layering is a very simple way of increasing the stocks for fruit crops such as strawberries and some herbs such as the mints and thymes. With strawberries, as the runners are produced, they can be either pinned in situ, using a bent piece of wire, or pinned into a pot of soil. Once the runner has rooted, it can be cut from the parent plant and the potted runner can be used immediately, whereas the one in the ground would have to be lifted and replanted in the winter or early spring when it is dormant. Layering herbs is much more straightforward, as they can be pinned down into the ground or a pot (as for strawberries) at any time, and they will root very quickly.

Repotting

When growing vegetables or herbs from seed or cuttings, it is important to keep them growing at their maximum rate. This means ensuring that they do not become root-bound in any container, whether it is a pot or an individual cell (plug). Many varieties of vegetables grown in cells can be planted outside directly from the tray, without the need for repotting. A few, however, and most of the herbs, will require growing in a pot before planting.

The main point to remember when repotting is not to overpot the plant, as too much wet soil around the root may cause it to rot. As an example, I would thin out tomato seedlings into 3-inch (8-cm) containers and then repot into a ½-gallon (2-liter), 1-gallon (5-liter), 1½-gallon (7½-liter), and finally a 2-gallon (10-liter) pot. Each potting should be carried out once the roots have nicely filled the sides of the pot but not started to curl around its bottom. It is also important to ensure the plants are getting enough feed from each pot they are put into. If you are using a proprietary organic potting soil, this should contain ample fertilizer to last the time the plant is in the pot. If using leaf mold or your own soil mix, this needs to be supplemented by some sort of organic feed. I either mix some pelleted chicken manure into the soil or use a proprietary seaweed complete liquid feed or homemade comfrey or nettle liquid feed.

The method used for repotting is quite simple. First, fill the new pot with soil to a level at which the top of the root ball of the plant being potted will finish just below the level of the new soil when the pot is filled. Position the plant in the pot so that it is sitting with the plant in the center. Do not worry if the roots are not centered—it is the top growth of the plant that needs to be in the center position. Loosely fill around the root ball with

soil until the pot is overfilled. Press the soil firmly around the roots once, using two or three fingers of each hand, and level off the soil to the top of the pot.

Once potted, the plants can be well watered. The art is to firm the soil enough so that it is pushed around the roots, but not so firmly that it is crammed in and goes as hard as concrete. Once watered a few times, the soil should sink just enough to leave a little lip between the top of the pot and the surface of the soil. This makes watering nice and easy, as the water does not instantly run off the soil and down the side of the pot. After watering, the pots can be labeled and the plants placed out, ensuring that they are spaced out enough so that they all receive good light and plenty of air movement. Air movement prevents a lot of the diseases associated with stagnant air and plants touching.

Many herbs, such as rosemary, pictured here, need to grow in pots before being planted in the garden.

Watering

Watering is definitely one of those jobs that is far harder than most people's perception of simply spraying water around. Timing is all-important.

Watering during Winter and Spring

The job of watering is very important in the late winter and early spring, as slightly too much water will cause crops to rot, while underwatering may cause a check in the crop growth, ultimately resulting in later harvesting. My philosophy when watering at this very precarious time is *if in doubt, don't*. Even though this may mean a slightly later harvest, you should always err on the side of caution—a later crop is by far better than one that has rotted in the greenhouse.

To counter this problem during the spring, I stand all my trays and pots on capillary matting, in the greenhouse. At least once a day, I water the matting to ensure it is kept wet, as the pots and trays will take up the water they require from this matting. It works, as the name suggests, through capillary action, with the drier soil drawing water from the wetter capillary mat. If the soil is not dry, it will not draw up any water, so there is no chance of plants rotting through overwatering using this method. It also limits the amount of overhead watering that is required, minimizing the potential for fungal diseases.

At this time of year, carry out all watering in the greenhouse with a watering can with a fine rose. Even with a fine rose, there is generally a sudden rush of water out of the can as it is tipped forward, before it stabilizes into a steady flow. Always start by holding the can away from the benches and move it over the seedlings once the initial rush of water has passed.

Due to the contrast between outside temperatures and greenhouse temperatures during spring, an indoor tank is a good idea. The indoor tank warms the water so that as the water is applied, the seedlings do not suffer a shock. I find a tank under the greenhouse benches awkward, so instead I ensure that there are always two full watering cans in the greenhouse—the water inside them quickly reaches the greenhouse temperature. After every watering, I refill them from the rain barrel outside. It is essential to have rain barrels positioned at the bottom of every gutter downspout, collecting water from all roof areas. Remember that these are not just a good store for fresh water, but can also be used to produce homemade liquid feed.

Watering during Warmer Weather

As the weather warms and the light levels increase, the plants' requirement for water becomes greater, at which point a medium rose can be used on the watering can, which will dispense more water. With warmer weather, there's less of a need for precise watering due to the increased evaporation from the soil surface and loss of water through the plant leaves. This does not mean that water can be applied without thought or care; it simply means that there is a little bit more leeway between watering with the right amount and overwatering. This is important because at some point the plants will require feeding, whether to encourage growth or for flowering and fruiting, and this is usually applied as a liquid feed when watering.

You have a little more leeway when watering plants in warm weather.

For crops grown outside, watering can be carried out using a watering can, hose, or sprinkler, but it is still as important to get the right amount of water onto the crops as when watering in the greenhouse. There will be more evaporation of water from the plant leaves as well as the soil surface, due not only to the summer heat but also to exposure to wind. Underwatering of maturing crops can result in those crops running to seed, producing hard and inedible produce, dropping a proportion of their fruit crop, or just ending up with a much-reduced yield, so the need for ample water is vital. The crops need to be started in the correct way, and applying water to the bottom of a shallow furrow before sowing will get the seeds germinating quickly and growing properly. Giving transplanted crops a good watering after planting will ensure that they do not wilt, but rather continue to grow unchecked, resulting in a bumper yield.

To ensure the produce is ready for harvest when planned, the crops must be kept growing at their optimum rate, which is why watering, particularly at stressful times for plants, is so essential. Once the crops have been sown or planted, there is no definitive timetable for applying water because each crop has different water needs, and the weather will not be consistent. It is important to be aware that windy or breezy and sunny days are very drying. All our productive areas are checked for watering every day.

Tips for Watering

If the productive area is small, all watering can be done by watering can, but on larger areas a hose will be easier as it saves a lot of walking to and fro. The good thing about a hose is that water can be applied exactly where it is needed, whereas when using a sprinkler, waste water falls in areas that are either unoccupied or not required by that crop. There are areas where the use of hoses and sprinklers is banned, so always check before using.

The most important factor when watering is to give the crops enough. A steady but constant watering that is allowed to penetrate deeper into the soil is by far better than a quick gush of water. Some of the latter will flow away and the rest wet only the very surface of the soil, where the water quickly evaporates in hot or windy weather.

For very precise watering on vegetable crops such as green (runner) beans, use either drip irrigation or a soaker hose. The drip irrigation needs to be run from a garden faucet, whereas a soaker hose can be run directly from a rain barrel. Both systems will deposit water where it is required and can be laid in place to last for the life of the crop.

Although watering is usually required on productive crops during most years, mulching and/or removing competition, such as weeds, minimizes its frequency.

Chapter 3

Organic Growing Methods

Early Crops

There is great value in harvesting some crops as early as possible, as this is the time when they are scarce and at their most expensive. It also gives mealtimes much more variety if early and late crops can be substituted for the more conventional winter varieties. There are several methods that can be employed in order to achieve this.

Hot Box

The hot-box method of using the heat given off by the rapid rotting of fresh horse manure has been used for many years as a means of obtaining early crops or being able to grow crops, such as pineapples, not usually suited to temperate climates. It is important to obtain the fresh horse manure from a stable that uses straw as a bedding material, as this will produce a much better heat than manure mixed with wood shavings. Microscopic bacteria break down the manure and straw at a very quick rate, thus generating heat; as wood is a much more fibrous material, rotting is much slower. The bacteria require nitrogen to feed on while they work on the process of breaking down the mixture of manure and straw, and, as urine found within this mix contains very high levels of nitrogen, their work rate is rapid. Heat will also help to increase the bacteria's work rate, and therefore the hot box should be constructed from four solid walls.

To maintain a good, consistent heat, the hot box should be constructed to a height of at least 3 feet (90 cm). The length and width are not vital; however, as there needs to be a cover placed over the top, I find that a box that is 7 feet (210 cm) long and 5 feet (150 cm) wide not only produces an ample harvest, but is also easy to manage. It is simple to construct and consists of four 66-inch (165-cm) long, 3-inch (8-cm) square wooden posts that are buried 18 inches (45 cm) into the ground. To these posts are nailed eight lengths of 6 x 1-inch (15 x 2½-cm) rough-sawn lumber, on one long side and the two ends. It is important to have removable boards on the remaining long side. Therefore, to

The hot box method utilizes heat from rotting horse manure.

the insides of each of these two posts are nailed two lengths of 1 x 1-inch (2½ x 2½-cm) battening. The side boards for this removable front are cut shorter so that they slide easily between the battens. There is no need for a solid bottom to the box.

I like to use the hot box for a crop of the earliest of early new potatoes, which are always harvested, come what may, on Easter Sunday. If Easter Sunday is early in the year, the harvested new potatoes resemble marbles, but when it falls at the end of April, the crop is absolutely fantastic!

Once there is enough fresh horse manure ready, usually by the first week of January, fill the hot box, firming lightly as you go. If the manure is overly compacted, the bacteria will not work to their best potential, so less heat will be generated; however, if it is not firmed at all, the heap will collapse very quickly and soon, quite literally, run out of steam. Make sure that you overfill the hot box so that the manure rises about 12 inches (30 cm) above the top of the box. Finally, top the fresh manure with a layer of well-rotted compost, soil, or proprietary compost to a depth of 6–8 inches (15–20 cm).

To gauge how much heat is being generated, push a 3-foot (90-cm) bamboo cane three-quarters of the way into the heap, so that occasionally it can be pulled out and

New potatoes are a good choice for an early crop.

touched, to determine the best time to plant the potatoes. Once you have topped the manure with the layer of compost, place a cloche or cold frame over the top of the hot box.

The box and its contents are then left for a minimum of two weeks, to allow the heap to cool just a fraction. If the potatoes are planted as soon as the box is filled, the heap will generate too much heat and cook the potatoes in situ, before they have a chance to grow. As an example of this, if the bamboo cane were to be removed from its position where it is pushed into the heap, after a week it would still not be possible to hold it for any length of time as it would be too hot.

After two weeks (usually the end of January), it is time to plant. There is no need to "chit" the potatoes prior to planting, as the heat will start them quickly into growth. I always plant the earliest variety of new potato in the hot box, generally a variety called 'Swift,' in order to get the earliest decent-sized potatoes possible by the harvest date. They are planted at a spacing of 6–8 inches (15–20 cm) and buried just below the soil level. If they are pushed in too deeply, they will be too close to the manure and will cook. After planting, the cloche is replaced on the top of the box and the tubers left to grow. Once the tubers start to produce visible shoots, the soil is topped up on a regular basis so that the resulting potatoes are covered and not exposed to the light.

All that is left to do is to check the potatoes regularly for water and keep topping up the soil as required. The heat generated from the heap and contained within our homemade cloche has kept out 21°F (–6°C) of frost. If low temperatures are forecast, however, extra protection is prudent, such as covering the tops with landscape, or garden, fabric or even newspaper to prevent any damage to these very frost-sensitive potato tops. The final task, on Easter Sunday, is to begin harvesting a lovely crop of new potatoes.

Once all the potatoes have been harvested from the hot box, remove the compost topping and then top up the box to its starting level with more fresh horse manure. Top with compost or soil as before and replace the cloche for another two weeks. Now you are ready to plant a crop more used to warmer temperatures, such as melons. Start them off under the cloche. Due to the ultimate cooler temperatures once the cloche has been removed, it is necessary to grow a variety that will tolerate this temperature regime, such as melon 'Sweetheart.' Once the daytime temperatures are reaching 70°F (21°C) permanently, remove the cloche. Without fail, year after year, we have been able to harvest melons grown in the hot box two weeks earlier than the same varieties grown in a heated greenhouse. They are therefore not only earlier, but also work out to be an awful lot cheaper than those grown in the greenhouse.

Once the melons have all been harvested, pull out the plants and remove the planks making up the front of the box to reveal a box of well-rotted farmyard manure that can be put straight onto the productive areas.

Mild Hot Bed

Although the hot box is a fantastic way of getting not only very early crops but also a container of well-rotted organic matter, it is not suitable for all because of the high temperatures reached. For those lower-temperature early crops a mild hot bed is ideal. Although both methods use absolutely fresh horse manure, the basic difference between a hot box and mild hot bed is that the latter is not enclosed in a box, but instead exposed to the elements. This means that the temperature of the manure will be lower, as the heat generated can escape and the lower outside temperatures will naturally lower the temperature within the heap.

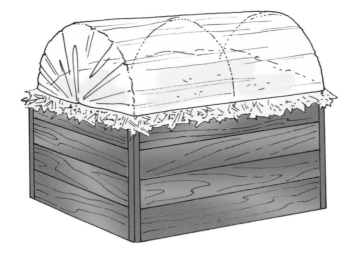

For the hot box at Barnsdale, we constructed a low tunnel, or cloche, that fits it perfectly.

To make a mild hot bed, pile the fresh manure into a flat heap about 3 feet (90 cm) high and cap with a 6–8-inch (15–20-cm) layer of compost or soil as before. Place a cloche or cold frame on top, and leave for two weeks to heat up. Once ready, it can be used for growing early salad crops such as lettuce, radish, scallion, multi-sown carrots, arugula (rocket), multi-sown beets (beetroot), and the like.

You will not get the largest of crops because of the restrictive size of the heap and the amount that can be grown under the cloche or cold frame, but nonetheless this approach is an integral part of a plan that will give a good continuity of early crops. Once the first batch of crops has been harvested, the heap can be topped up as many times as required or until the supply of fresh horse manure is exhausted. At the end of the growing season, the well-rotted pile of manure can be spread as before.

Heating

Early crops can be given the best start possible by germinating them on some sort of basal heat. This may involve the use of a propagator, for smaller amounts. An electric propagator is a simple device, where a heated base is topped by a removable plastic dome-shaped lid. A thermostat regulates the basal temperature to give the ideal temperature for the seed being germinated. Propagators come in many different sizes, ranging from ones that can accommodate only one seed tray to much larger devices that will cope with up to twelve standard seed trays.

If you need to propagate more seed trays at one time than the propagator allows, there are two basic options for heating seed trays from below. The easiest way is with a heated mat, whereby electric cables have been sealed in matting that can be rolled out whenever required and plugged in, with a fitted thermostat to regulate the temperature. Once the seeds have been germinated, the matting can be rolled up and put away until it is required again. A more permanent method is to use coated electric cables, laid out in a layer of coarse sand at the required spacing and then covered with another layer of coarse sand. Again, a thermostat regulates the temperature.

Both of these methods will give seeds the fastest start to obtain not only the earliest crops but also better control of the continuity of some crops, which can be erratic and slower if germination is done without heat.

It is also possible to germinate seeds in warmer parts of the house, such as a laundry room or linen closet with a water heater in it. It is warm and usually has built-in shelves for the pots or seeds to sit on, and it works very well. The main problem is that it is dark, so as soon as there is any sign of germination, the seed tray or pot needs to be moved immediately to a light place. This could be a greenhouse, a conservatory, or even the kitchen windowsill. If the seedlings are placed on the latter, be careful of nighttime temperatures, which can affect young and tender seedlings. Although the seedlings will not freeze on the windowsill, the temperatures can drop very low.

Although a windowsill provides light, the temperature can drop after the sun goes down.

Seedlings need to be turned regularly, as they bend toward the light, with the turning of seed trays and pots giving the seedlings an even supply of light, preventing them from becoming leggy as they reach for the sunlight. To counter this problem, you can make a simple but very effective growing box that will reflect the light all around the seedlings, eliminating the need for constant turning. The basic requirements for this are a cardboard box and either white gloss paint or foil. The size of the box is unimportant, but will be regulated by the size of the windowsill on which it will sit. Cut one of the longest sides of the box, leaving a 2-inch (5-cm) strip at the base, then cut a diagonal from each of the opposite corners down to this strip.

The whole of the inside of the box can be painted with the white gloss or lined with foil. It is now ready for use and works by reflecting the incoming light off the back and sides of the box and onto the seedlings, giving an all-around light effect. While this simple system will provide all the light that is needed to produce strong seedlings, you will need a stronger, more substantial structure to get the earliest crops.

Tomato seedlings enjoy the warmth of a greenhouse when outside temperatures are low.

Using a Greenhouse or Conservatory

Extra care is necessary to keep seedlings growing at their maximum during the early, colder parts of the season. There is no question that, to obtain the earliest crops from most vegetable varieties, this can be achieved only when using a greenhouse or conservatory. It is crucial that when seeds are germinated early, the resulting seedlings and plants can be grown without fear of the outside temperature. This fear is also greatly diminished if the greenhouse or conservatory is heated. It need not have a fancy heating system, as most early vegetable varieties will simply require frost-free protection. The more tender crops such as cucumbers, melons, and tomatoes, however, will require a minimum temperature of 60°F–70°F (15°C–21°C).

Overturned mason jars make good cloches.

Early Crops Outside

The main aim with early crops grown outside is to keep them growing and not to check that growth in any way. Therefore, when the plants are ready to be planted, the ground has to be ready. If you are gardening on a light or sandy soil, this is not usually a problem. This type of soil, by its nature, will usually remain dry and not become waterlogged, and therefore warm up quickly. This is not the case with heavy or clay soils, as they tend to retain moisture, usually to the point where they are unworkable during the early, wetter part of the growing season. It is this wetness in colder weather that keeps the soil cold and unsuitable for early crops.

To ensure that the required ground is ready for the plants when the plants are ready for it, the soil should be covered. It is important to cover the soil into which these early crops will be planted as early as possible, ideally early winter, so that the soil's moisture content can be regulated. Cover the soil with a sheet of plastic (preferably black, but clear would do) or by using cloches. This covering keeps off unwanted rain and also warms the soil, so that the soil is in perfect condition just when those early crops need it and not when the weather dictates that they can be planted. This method also highlights the importance of planning. Coverings can be placed where the early crops are to be grown, rather than the crops having to be grown in the only piece of covered ground.

Small Victorian cloches in a vegetable garden.

Once these early crops have been planted, they usually have to be protected from the worst of the late winter/early spring weather. A lot of this protection is given by using different structures. These can be plastic hoophouse cloches, rigid cloches, bell jars, cold frames, plastic soda bottles, or Victorian-style cloches.

All of these structures are readily obtained, but some are very easy to make and will last just as long for a fraction of the price. As they are movable, they can be used wherever they are required in the productive plot, then moved onto the next area without any significant problems. Bell jars and Victorian-style cloches are also very ornamental and therefore much more pleasing to the eye than plastic cloches; however, due to their size they can be used to cover only a very small quantity of crop and are expensive to purchase. As all of these structures are impenetrable by rain, watering will need to be carried out as and when required.

Garden fabric, or row cover, is a product that can be used for early crops, as it is a light woven material that can be laid flat over a crop. The fact that it is woven is very important, as it is the air spaces between the woven threads that trap the air, which has an insulating effect on the crops below. For this insulator to work effectively, it must lie directly on the crop and not be supported above it, where all the insulating properties are lost. This is not usually a problem as it is a light material, although it is obviously heavier when it gets wet, which can be a problem on some of the more delicate crops. Still, this is a minor problem when you consider how much frost protection you get.

You really need to peg down the edges of the fabric or bury its edges in the soil to keep it in place, particularly on windy sites. When secured well to the ground, it also protects crops from flying insects such as aphid, carrot root fly, and whitefly. The great asset of this material is that it is water and air permeable; as such, you usually can leave it in place, sometimes for the life of the crop. The only problem that may occur is on bright spring days, when there may be some scorching to the edges of larger-leaved plants where they are in contact with the fabric.

Year-Round Potatoes

There is something very special about harvesting the first crop of new potatoes just as most gardeners are planting theirs. The trick is to keep them going until the earliest of the first earlies planted outside are ready. My tried-and-tested method keeps us in potatoes all year round.

As we plant the hot box with potato 'Swift,' we also put some into a large container of our well-rotted compost. The container is 30 inches (75 cm) across and holds six tubers. At the same time, we plant other pots with first early potatoes, such as 'Lady Christi' or 'Rocket,' which will mature later than the 'Swift.' It is important to vary the varieties so that no two varieties mature at the same time. These are left under the bench in a heated greenhouse. The next three containers planted in the same way are grown in an unheated greenhouse, so that they will naturally mature slightly later than the first batch. In mid-March, three rows of carefully selected first early potatoes are planted outside, again using 'Swift' as one of the varieties, to ensure a succession. These three rows are then covered with clear plastic. Next to these are planted the remaining first earlies, then the second earlies and, two weeks later, all the main-crop potatoes.

The first early potatoes planted under the plastic will mature faster than those in open ground, as the plastic heats the ground and brings on the crop underneath. I like to use clear plastic, as it is then possible to see the emerging potato tops, while still keeping all the heat and moisture in the ground. As the potatoes grow, their tops start to push up against the plastic. Cut a small cross just above each of them to allow the tops to be pulled through. The plants and the plastic are then left until it is time to harvest, when the plastic is lifted and removed as each variety is dug up.

You can use black plastic to cover the early outdoor crop, but this must be in place and dug in before the crop is planted. A cross is then cut into the plastic at the correct planting distance; the tubers are planted through it and into the ground. This method is better at keeping the weeds at bay, but when the shoots do start to emerge, if they do not come up exactly where the crosses have been cut and they are not quickly maneuvered through the holes, they suffer from lack of light. This may delay the crop or even reduce the harvest if it happens a lot. It is true that there will be a decent crop of weeds under the clear plastic, but they do stay under the plastic and they should be regarded as an excellent green manure crop that can be dug in when the potatoes are harvested.

These covered first early potatoes will follow the container ones, and when they have all been dug up, the natural progression is onto the first early varieties planted in open ground next to them. These are followed by the second earlies, then the main-crop varieties. The bulk of the main-crop potatoes are harvested and the perfect ones bagged and put into storage for use through the winter. They will last until the following spring, when the hot-box first earlies are ready and the whole cycle begins again.

Its uses are not limited simply to bringing on and protecting early crops. Row-cover fabric can also be used to protect later crops that would not usually require any protection. For instance, it has been known that a light frost at night has been forecast in early June, just after the outdoor tomatoes have been planted. In this case, the easiest method of protecting the crop is to throw row cover over all of the plants during late afternoon and remove it in the morning. This product is capable of keeping out enough frost to prevent those early crops from becoming damaged. It is not infallible, though, and if the weather turns unseasonably cold, the plants will require extra protection.

Fabric that has been used to protect early crops from the cold and is no longer required can be held over the hoops of a grow tunnel and used as a barrier to protect crops against flying insects.

Training and Pruning Fruit

Training Soft Fruit

There are several methods of training soft fruit, although there are some that will produce happily without the need for training, as long as they are maintained correctly.

Raspberries, Hybrid Berries, and Blackberries

On our community-garden area at Barnsdale, we grow the raspberries, hybrid berries, and blackberries in rows, tied to long runs of strong galvanized wires that are attached to tall fence posts. Usually we use 8-foot (2⅖-m) posts, with 18–24 inches (45–60 cm) being knocked into the ground. The galvanized wire is attached every 24 inches (60 cm), which gives three strands onto which the canes can be tied, using soft garden twine. For main-crop or summer-fruiting raspberries, the fruiting canes are tied to the wires, while the canes that grow during that fruiting season are left untied

A raspberry cane with berries ready to be picked.

until the raspberries have been picked. The raspberry canes that have fruited are then cut down to ground level, and the canes that grew during the summer are tied in to fruit during the following summer.

While autumn-fruiting varieties are often self-supporting, the outer canes may need support. A simple system of four posts, one in each corner, and a single strand of wire enclosing the whole bed of canes will suffice. Because the fruits are produced on the current year's growth, all of the canes can be cut right down to ground level once the crop has fruited. Hybrid berries and blackberries are trained on the same supports as raspberries, but in a slightly different manner because of their vigor. Tie all of the fruiting shoots onto the supporting wires on one side of the plant; as the new shoots grow throughout the summer, train them onto the wires on the opposite side of the plant. Once fruiting has finished, as for summer-fruiting raspberries, cut out the fruited canes, leaving space for the next year's canes to be tied in.

Red and White Currants

When it comes to red currants and white currants, these can be easily grown in most gardens as freestanding bushes. By training them up a fence, a wall, or wires, however, you can grow them in a much more restricted space and make them infinitely more interesting to look at. They look particularly good grown as cordons or in a fan shape.

Currants are easy to grow as freestanding bushes.

Training Currants into Cordons or Fans

Training a cordon currant is simple, with the bushes planted so that their "arms" are always 12 inches (30 cm) apart. Therefore, single-cordon plants are planted 12 inches (30 cm) apart, double cordons are planted 24 inches (60 cm) apart, triple cordons planted 36 inches (90 cm) apart, and so on. Buy the currants as young plants so that they can be initially pruned and trained in this way. The fence or wall needs to be wired so that there is something in place to which to tie the stems. Position the wires horizontally and spaced about 12 inches (30 cm) apart. Fan-trained plants should be planted about 6 feet (1⁴/₅ m) apart with five or six arms tied onto wire at an even spacing between them.

For a single-stem cordon, you must obtain a one-year-old plant with just the single stem; this stem is trained directly upward or at an angle of 45 degrees to the ground. Tie the stem into place and, as it grows, tie in accordingly. With the double cordons, triple cordons, and fans, you can buy a two-year-old plant and then select and tie in the appropriate stems and completely remove all of the other stems. The other method is to buy a one-year-old single stem and prune it as desired. As the lateral stems grow out from the main stem, tie in the required shoots and remove any that are not required. As the shoots grow, tie in accordingly.

With multibranched cordons, the fruiting shoots are trained vertically. If training onto a post-and-wire system, as used for raspberries, blackberries, and hybrid berries, the posts and wires can be positioned so that they act as a wind barrier for the rest of the productive area.

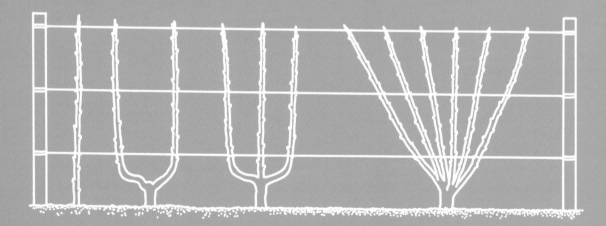

Because they are prone to winter damage during severe winters, red currants and white currants should always be pruned in late winter or early spring. This means that you will be able to remove any winter damage suffered. If grown as a freestanding bush, both of these varieties can be spur-pruned to encourage fruiting spurs to form on the main stems.

The aim is always to create an open, goblet-shaped bush. This can be achieved by removing all the congested, older branches, as well as the crossing and weak branches. All the remaining side shoots are then cut back to two or three buds. When pruning all types of cordon, there are two stages of pruning. The first is at the same time as for bush-grown plants, when all the weak spur systems, as well as diseased and congested branches, are removed. The remainder of the pruning is left until summer, so that the plant's growth can be restricted. Cut back all the side shoots to five leaves, which will improve air circulation around the plants, thus minimizing the risk of disease as well as removing any pests present on the shoot tips and of course restricting the

growth of each cordon. For fan-trained plants, once the shape has been formed, all spur pruning is carried out in winter or early spring as for a bush.

Gooseberries

Gooseberries can be trained in several ways, adding some really interesting shapes to the productive garden. They can be grown as a bush, single-stem cordon, double cordon, triple cordon, fan, or standard. The main method used in the productive garden is as a bush, where they are grown as a freestanding plant on a single stem. These bushes can be bought as such or hardwood cuttings taken from another bush and the bush produced from that. If growing single, double, or triple cordons and fans, these are trained in exactly the same way as for red and white currants.

Ripe berries on a gooseberry bush.

With some carefully planned pruning, this grapevine could be even more productive.

The more complicated but probably most ornamental training method is that of a standard. It is possible to buy these already trained and ready to go, but they can also be trained from either a rooted cutting or a cordon stem. The advantage of buying a plant that has already been trained is that the bush at the top of the long stem will produce gooseberries in its first season; if you train one up from a cutting, it will be several seasons before it is productive. Doing it yourself is by far the more satisfying way, however, with the single-stem option a bit of a fast-track method. A standard gooseberry does not want to have a stem longer than 3 feet (90 cm), as a longer stem would not be able to support the weight of the head. At the 3-foot (90-cm) point, cut the stem so that the buds are encouraged to grow out and produce the required head, from which the fruits are produced. Each year, this head will increase until the desired size is achieved.

For plants grown as bushes or standards, pruning is carried out immediately after the crop has been harvested, when all the side shoots are cut back to five leaves. Also remove any diseased and congested branches at this time. When pruning cordons and fan-trained gooseberries, prune back all the side shoots at the same time and in the same way, down to only 3 inches (8 cm) from the base. Prune back all secondary shoots coming off the remaining side shoots to 1 inch (2½ cm) from their base.

Black Currants

Black currants fruit best on one-year-old shoots, which makes them unsuitable for growing in any form other than bush. When planting a black currant bush, put it into the prepared hole so that it is 2 inches (5 cm) lower than the level of the top of the pot or the original soil level at which it was grown, if the plant is bare root. If planted in this way, the bush can be "stooled," which involves cutting half the branches down to soil level every year. The bush will fruit on the half that remains, while the new shoots emerge from below soil level. That autumn, cut back all the shoots that have fruited to soil level, leaving the new shoots in place. Using this method produces a two-year cycle, so that half the bush is fruiting every year. When starting to prune using this method, do not initially cut down all the branches on one side, so that the bush looks lopsided; select branches throughout the bush so that after you remove half, you are left with a nicely open bush, not an eyesore.

Grapes

Grapes are becoming quite a popular crop to grow outdoors. As varieties have improved, this option has become eminently possible in temperate areas. It used to be the case that most temperate areas were restricted to growing grapes for winemaking, but edible grapes are now a viable crop in most years.

For a good crop of juicy, sweet grapes, train the vine against a south-facing wall or a post-and-wire support in a sheltered area. After planting, cut the solitary main shoot back hard to leave only three good, healthy buds. In the first year, tie the resulting three vertical shoots onto the wires and cut back all side shoots to five or six leaves. Once the leaves have dropped and the plant is dormant, pull down the two outer stems so that they lay horizontal, about 18 inches (45 cm) from ground level, and at an angle of 90 degrees to the remaining shoot. Cut back the remaining vertical shoot again to three good, healthy buds.

To ensure the fruits ripen at the end of the season, allow only the vertical shoots to grow up 30 inches (75 cm) from the horizontal stems, at which point the tips should be removed. Remove all side shoots that appear on these vertical shoots, and allow only one bunch of grapes to develop on each shoot. During the growing season, remove any leaves that shade the developing fruits. The three shoots that arise from the central vertical shoot that you cut back the previous winter should be tied in vertically; you will use these shoots to replace the shoots tied in the previous winter.

Once the crop has been harvested and the leaves have fallen from the plant, cut out the two horizontal branches that carried the fruiting verticals completely; tie in the two outer verticals of the group of three shoots rising from the center buds to replace them. It is important to prune shoots only in winter, when the plant is dormant, as they bleed profusely during the growing season. Carry out only essential tipping of young shoots and side shoots during the growing season.

Training Fruit Trees

It is important to understand that there is an inextricable link between training fruit trees, such as apple, pear, peach, nectarine, plum, cherry, apricot, and fig, and the pruning of these fruits. The required shape of a tree totally dictates the way in which it is pruned. If carried out regularly, as it should be, pruning of fruit trees will require only the use of a pair of pruning shears, pruning saw, loppers, and a ladder. Where there is an old and uncared-for tree to prune, you may need long-handled loppers or even a chainsaw.

When growing these fruit trees, training is carried out in one of various ways. Some fruit types respond well to more than one method, while others only perform well if trained in one particular way. The training methods are:

- bush
- half-standard
- standard
- pyramid
- festooned
- cordon

- oblique cordon
- "U" cordon
- double "U" cordon
- espalier
- stepover
- fan
- lollipop

Bush

This is likely to be the most popular method of training a freestanding fruit tree because the tree remains small and manageable, with fruit picking being carried out without the use of a ladder. The tree is generally purchased when it is under four years old, either as a single-stem one-year-old whip or a partially trained two- or three-year-old tree. Pruning in the early years of any bush is carried out during winter, when the tree is dormant, because all pruning is directed toward creating the perfect shape. The ideal is to create a wineglass shape so that there is plenty of air circulation through the tree to minimize the risk of disease to the tree and the fruits. This shape will also ensure that the middle is open and not congested, which helps by allowing maximum light into the tree to aid ripening.

Training Fruit Trees

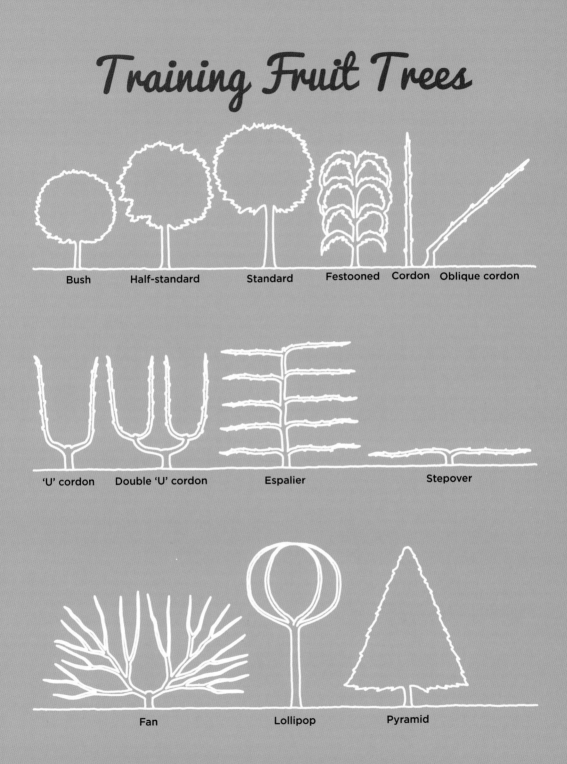

Bush   Half-standard   Standard   Festooned   Cordon   Oblique cordon

'U' cordon   Double 'U' cordon   Espalier   Stepover

Fan   Lollipop   Pyramid

During winter, remove all unwanted shoots and cut the remaining ones back by about two-thirds each time. Ensure that each cut is made to an outward-facing bud. Before every cut is made, it is important to determine in what direction the resulting shoot will grow; shoots that grow into the tree and ones that will cause congestion or cross over other established shoots must be avoided. If the bud at two-thirds is not a good one, then cut to the nearest outward-facing bud. It is far more important to have the shoots growing in the right direction than worrying about whether the cut made will leave the shoot slightly longer or shorter than suggested.

Once the shape has been formed, usually after four years, pruning switches to promoting fruiting instead of growth. This is where tree variety comes into play, as apples and pears are divided into two pruning groups: tip bearers ('Bramley's Seedling,' 'Discovery,' and 'Worcester Pearmain') and spur bearers (all other varieties).

Tip bearers fruit on one-year-old wood, while spur bearers will fruit on two- to three-year-old wood. It is important to know which category your tree falls into so that the following year's fruiting wood is not removed.

Winter pruning of spur bearers consists of cutting away any diseased wood, crossing branches, and unwanted branches and thinning spurs as required. Summer pruning consists of pruning as for a cordon.

Tip bearers need to be lightly pruned in the winter. Slightly cut back the tips so as not to remove too many fruit buds. Remove any unproductive, overcrowded, crossing, or diseased branches. Any side shoots less than 12 inches (30 cm) long are left.

Half-Standard and Standard

These are bush trees that are grown on a taller main stem, with the half-standard generally having the head starting at the top of a 4-foot (1⅓-m) stem and the standard at the top of a 6-foot (1⅘-m) stem. The pruning of the head is the same as for a bush.

Pyramid

For pyramid training on young trees, usually younger than four years old, every summer cut the tips of each of the five or six evenly spaced branches you have selected back to 6 inches (15 cm) of the current year's growth. Prune the side shoots to 4 inches (10 cm) and any secondary shoots to 2 inches (5 cm). Each winter, prune the leading shoot on the opposite side from the previous year to 8 inches (20 cm) of the previous season's growth. Once the tree has reached the required height and spread, prune back twice as hard:

Main shoots	2¾ inches (7 cm)
Side shoots	2 inches (5 cm)
Secondary shoots	1 inch (2½ cm)

Cordon/Oblique Cordon

As the tree is maturing, in summer prune the side shoots to 2¾ inches (7 cm) from the main stem and secondary shoots to 1 inch (2½ cm). In winter, prune the leader by one-third of that year's growth. Once the end of the cane has been reached, cut the side shoots back to 1 inch (2½ cm) from the previous year's growth or the first true leaf. In winter, prune to ease congestion.

Festooned

The tree is trained like this to restrict growth and thus encourage better fruiting. Prune each shoot as for cordon training.

Espalier

When the tree is forming, cut in winter to three buds—two for laterals and one for leader—18–24 inches (45–60 cm) from the ground, then repeat for each tier. Once the height has been reached, make a final cut to two buds and train out laterals. When established, prune laterals as for a cordon.

Stepover

The training method for the stepover is as per the espalier, only first cut to two buds and train along wire 12 inches (30 cm) from the ground. Prune laterals as for a cordon.

A productive espalier-trained pear tree.

Apple trees respond well to lollipop training.

Lollipop

This is a training method that we used at Barnsdale in the 1990s, and the tree has really stood the test of time, reaching no more than 7 feet (a little more than 2 m). If a "family" apple or pear tree is used, where three or preferably four different varieties are grafted onto one stem, you'll need only one tree because each of these varieties will pollinate at least one of the others. Taking this into account, there is no reason why every garden cannot have at least one apple or pear tree. It is a very simple method, using a one-year-old whip that will be a single-variety tree or a two- to three-year-old tree that could be either a family or single-variety type.

If using a one-year-old whip, cut the stem above four good buds at the point where the head is required to start. As these shoots grow, tie them into a circular framework made from polyethylene pipe. The framework consists of two pieces of pipe, one slightly shorter than the other so that it fits inside the first once both are made into circles. To make them into circles, insert a 6-inch (15-cm) piece of cane into one end and push the other end of the pipe over the piece of cane sticking out. Tie the two pipes together in the centers of the circles, and use a strong wire to hold them in place.

As each of the shoots grows, treat as an individual cordon and prune accordingly. Once the shoots meet at the top of the circles, cut the shoots to an upward-facing bud and train the last shoot upward into a spur. After three to four years, when the tree is able to maintain its own shape without being tied in, remove the polyethylene pipe.

The method is the same if using a two- to three-year-old tree, except that initially four good branches are selected for training around the frame and all the others removed completely. The frame can also be made with strong wire and would need to be modified slightly if using a three-variety family tree.

◆ ◆ ◆ ◆

Apples and pears are the most versatile fruit trees, and the ones that can be trained in all of the aforementioned styles. Plums, cherries, peaches, nectarines, and apricots are usually grown as half-standards, standards, or fans. In temperate climates, peaches, nectarines, and apricots generally perform better when fan-trained. Figs are grown as fans, both inside and out.

Pruning Fruit Trees

For apples and pears, pruning is carried out at two distinct times of the year. Winter pruning encourages the tree to grow, so is primarily used to shape the tree in its formative years, although there will be a small amount of pruning to maintain the tree during this period. Summer pruning encourages the tree to form fruiting buds and is used once the shape of the tree has been created.

Cherry trees are pruned in spring to minimize the risk of fatal disease.

With other trees, such as plums, cherries, peaches, nectarines, and apricots, all pruning is carried out in the spring, just as the trees start into growth. This is not to control growth or fruiting, as is the case for apples and pears, but to minimize the risk of infection from silver leaf and bacterial canker. Both of these diseases can be fatal to these trees, so it is important to prune only when the wounds will heal quickly. If the tree is pruned in winter, the cuts will take a long time to heal over and stand much more chance of being infected by the windblown spores of these diseases. When training a young plum or cherry tree, it is best to prune during late March and April. Once the shape has been achieved, the tree's pruning is kept to a minimum. This usually involves cutting out dead, diseased, and crossing branches to keep the head nice and open.

Prune standard and half-standard trees during late June and July to keep them healthy. Remove any unwanted shoots to ease overcrowding and to allow in more light. On fan-trained trees, prune at the same time as for standards by pinching out all side shoots to six leaves, then cut the shoots back by half after fruiting. Try to prune to a triple bud, as it is very difficult to distinguish between vegetative and fruiting buds. You can almost guarantee a good crop of fruiting buds by doing it this way.

Peaches, nectarines, and apricots grown as standards are pruned in the same way as plums and cherries, in that they are thinned during late June or July. Whether you are

A fig tree, *Ficus carica*.

training the tree as a standard or a fan, always prune back
to a growth bud and not a fruiting bud, and if necessary
prune to a triple bud and remove the two fruiting buds.
If you are growing the tree as a fan, carry out the first
pruning in late March or early April, as the tree bursts
into growth. Choose a replacement shoot near the base
of each of the shoots chosen to fruit that year and one
a bit farther up. Tie the replacement shoot to the wire or
trellis supports to allow maximum light into the fan, helping
with ripening of the fruit.

The next job is to cut back all remaining shoots on the tree
to one leaf, which will help feed the tree and ensure all effort is
channeled into the fruit produced. After picking, in midsummer, cut
back all the shoots that have borne fruit to the tied-in replacement shoot,
and also cut out any dead or diseased wood. Peaches, nectarines, and apricots are
generally grown as fan-trained trees on south-facing walls in temperate climates, so
that they get enough sun and heat to produce a reliable crop each year.

In temperate climates, figs are generally grown against a protected wall or fence,
although in very sheltered areas they can be grown as bush trees. When a fig is grown
against a wall or fence, there need to be wire supports in place to tie the branches to,
and these need to be spaced about 12 inches (30 cm) apart. There is no need to prune
the fig in order to obtain the fan shape, as this can be created simply by tying branches
and shoots into the correct place. The spacing between branches and shoots should
be approximately 9 inches (23 cm). In order to maintain the shape of both growing
methods and ensure ripening of fruits, the figs require pruning in early spring when the
worst of the severe frosts has passed.

Figs are vigorous growers and, left to their own devices, would produce much more
growth than fruits, with the branches quickly becoming old, woody, and less productive.
You therefore need to be quite severe when pruning and remove a quarter of the oldest
wood of an established tree every spring; this ensures that the whole tree is renewed
every four years. Make each cut to within 2–3 inches (5–8 cm) of the base, so as to leave
a stump from which new, young shoots will grow. At the same time, remove any crossing
branches and branches growing into the tree, as well as tying in the remaining shoots.
The pruning of a freestanding tree is identical, but be careful when selecting branches
to be removed, in order to maintain the shape of the head.

Raised Beds

There are four basic reasons for growing crops in raised beds:

- to improve drainage
- to grow plants in a different soil
- for easy reach
- for earlier crops

A raised bed is a structure constructed on the surface of the ground and filled with substrate in order to grow fruit, flowers, vegetables, or herbs. The material used to make raised beds can vary greatly but in the end will do the job required of it. There is no blueprint as to how high or wide the bed should be; these dimensions are usually down to a combination of personal preference and the crop to be grown.

Wooden Raised Beds

If using wood to construct the bed, the dimensions should not really be any less than 5 inches (12½ cm) x 1 inch (2½ cm). We have found that the centers of beds 4 feet (120 cm) wide are easily reachable by most people, so this is the standard width we use at Barnsdale. The length of a raised bed is totally up to the person using it and how far he or she is prepared to walk in order to get around to the other side. Bear in mind that the farthest distance will be from the center of the bed on one side to the center of the bed on the other.

When considering wood for an organic garden, remember that you cannot use chemically treated wood because it has been impregnated with chemicals in order to lengthen the wood's life. This means there are really two options: you can either use the wood in its natural, raw state or treat it with an organically approved wood preservative. Unless you are concerned about the finished look, use sawn lumber rather than the planed alternative, as this will be considerably cheaper.

The wood is kept upright by being nailed or screwed to stakes, knocked into the ground on the inside of the bed. Having the stakes on the inside keeps them hidden by the soil, making the beds more aesthetically pleasing to the eye, as well as preventing any tripping problems. If attaching the wood to the stakes with nails, it is better to use annular ring nails as these will not pull out under the weight of soil.

The pathways between the beds need to be just wide enough to be able to work from and walk down pushing a wheelbarrow, so 12 inches (30 cm) should be just

You must not use chemically treated wood for organic raised beds.

about right. Remember that the wider the path, the more essential raised bed space is being taken up, resulting in a lower potential crop for the whole area.

Once the bed has been constructed, the soil should be double-dug, which can be done by digging down the bed. This initial digging should be the last time anybody's foot is allowed to stand on the bed. It is important that the soil structure is maintained and that no compaction of any sort occurs, so all work is carried out from the pathways on either side of the bed. This is why it is important to be able to easily reach the center of the bed; if 4 feet (120 cm) is too wide, make the beds slightly narrower. Each year, the bed can be double-dug, single-dug, or just tilled, depending on the crop to be grown. Because there is no need for long rows, as most plants will be grown in staggered rows across the beds, and all the plants can be reached from the pathways, there is no need to have room between each row down which to walk. This means that crops will be grown at a closer spacing, therefore producing a bigger harvest for the area used.

Other Types of Raised Beds

There are other materials besides wood that can also be used very effectively as edging for raised beds. Everybody will have something that they prefer, but there are far too many to mention them all.

Railroad Ties

Railroad ties tend to be treated with either tar or creosote and cannot be bought for use in the garden. It is possible to buy new landscape timbers, which are made to the same dimensions from new wood, having never seen a railroad line! These new timbers are very often treated wood; however, inquire before purchasing. They make excellent raised beds, usually having dimensions of 9 inches (23 cm) x 6 inches (15 cm), and can stand directly on the soil surface or at a higher level by stacking one on top of the other. If stacking timbers, you will need to attach wood between them to secure them.

When using a very deep bed, it is always worth ensuring there is somewhere for the excess water to pass out of the bed. Do this either by cultivating the soil at the original ground level, so that excess water can filter away in this direction, or by making sure that the bed's edging is not too tightly sealed, allowing excess water to pass out gradually through the joints in the timbers.

Raised Beds without Edging

You can also create a raised bed with no edging at all, using careful soil placement and string lines to keep it symmetrical. The soil will be naturally raised by the addition of organic matter, with the soil between the beds, used as paths, sinking slightly as it becomes compacted.

Round Fence Posts

Round fence posts, with a minimum 2- to 3-inch (5- to 8-cm) diameter, can be cut up into the lengths required. Allow about 18 inches (45 cm) can be buried in the ground to ensure the bed's edging is secure and does not move under the weight of soil.

This depth is adequate for beds up to 24 inches (60 cm) high, but taller beds will need to have the posts buried deeper into the ground. Buy the posts from a lumberyard because that is where you are most likely to find untreated posts.

Placing bricks horizontally in rows is just one way to use bricks for a raised bed.

Synthetic Wood

Synthetic wood is becoming more and more available. It is made from recycled plastic and looks very effective. It can be nailed, cut, and even planed like real wood but obviously lasts much longer. Beds are constructed in the same way as for sawn lumber.

Bricks

Bricks can be used in several ways, although their use tends to mean permanent beds rather than ones that can easily be chopped and changed at a later date. If the bricks are going to be laid flat and mortared into layers, the final height of bed is endless, as long as there has been a proper footing put in place. When constructing our asparagus raised beds, we also wanted to make an ornamental feature of them, so we made them 36 inches (90 cm) tall. I also find bricks laid at a 45-degree angle very effective, and these can be held in place just with the soil, although they will move fractionally over time. To keep them totally in place, they would need to be set in mortar. A variation on this theme is to lay the brick vertically, which gives a slightly higher bed than if set at an angle.

Soil in Raised Beds

Once you've constructed the beds, you need to turn your attention to the soil. Lower raised beds can have the soil improved as previously mentioned, with the deeper beds having to be filled with a growing medium. Because we garden in a heavy clay soil, I like to use equal parts soil, compost, and gravel (coarse grit) as the deep-bed growing medium. The soil gives the mix body, while the garden compost or well-rotted farmyard manure helps to retain moisture and also adds some nutrients; the gravel keeps the mix fairly open so that excess water can easily drain away. I have found that a pea-sized gravel does the job adequately. Remember when filling these deeper beds that the soil will sink slightly, so have some mix ready to top up with.

   As mentioned right at the start, raised beds, by the sheer nature of raising the soil, will have a much better drainage than the surface soil. It is also easier to manipulate the soil in order to obtain the right soil for the crops being grown. Another advantage is that the layout of these beds and the minimal use of pathways mean there will be more yield for the area used than there would be if growing in the traditional row system. Finally, for gardeners such as us who have a heavy clay soil in which to grow all of our produce, raising the height of the soil and improving drainage give us a much earlier crop than growing in wet and cold surface soil, as the drier soil warms up more quickly.

Tiles

Tiles that are specially made for the purpose tend to be either Victorian in style or very modern. As with bricks, they can be set in the soil or in mortar, and also do not give a great depth of soil above the original soil surface. This style should be seen primarily as a decorative feature because to obtain a decent depth of soil above the original level the tiles would really need to be three times the size.

Bamboo

In the right situation, bamboo roll or larger bamboo poles cut into lengths can be used and set in the ground using the same principles as for fence posts. It would probably give somewhat of a Japanese feel to the area, so would be limited in its use.

Woven Willow or Hazel

Woven willow or hazel gives a lovely old-fashioned look to beds but does not last very long—maybe only two or three seasons—when used to contain soil. It would be far better, if you want to achieve this look, to make the beds out of a longer-lasting material and surround it with the willow or hazel.

Concrete

I would not use concrete blocks, slabs, or paving stones in our raised beds at Barnsdale, as they do not fit into the look of our productive gardens; however, they do make excellent raised beds and will last a lifetime. They are all very heavy, and thus require setting into the soil or mortar in an adequate way so that there is no risk of them falling over and causing injury.

Wine Bottles

For anybody who is a wine aficionado, overturned wine bottles make a very decorative edging for raised beds. They are quite tough and will take knocks and bumps to a point, but, once broken, they are obviously very dangerous and would need to be replaced immediately.

Protected Crops

There is a range of fruiting vegetables that produce a much better crop, when being grown in a temperate climate, with the protection of a greenhouse or polyethylene tunnel/hoophouse. These do not need to be heated for the length of the growing season but will need heat during the early colder months in order to get the crop started. All of these protected crops can be sown during February, in a heated greenhouse or conservatory, giving the optimum time over which fruit can be harvested. The main fruiting vegetables grown under protection in temperate climates are tomatoes, cucumbers, melons, peppers, and eggplant (aubergines). If the correct growing and training techniques are implemented for these vegetables, bumper crops can certainly be achieved.

Tomatoes

I like to start sowing my first tomatoes into seed trays in January, and I continue to sow until the end of February, which ensures a good early fruiting as well as later fruits from

Certain crops benefit from the warmth of a hoophouse in colder weather.

the later sowing. Until they are ready for planting, the tomatoes require a minimum temperature of 70°F (21°C). At the first true leaf stage, thin out the seedlings into 3-inch (8-cm) pots. Each time the roots of the plants form around the soil in the pot, repot in stages into a ½-gallon (2-liter), 1-gallon (5-liter), 1½-gallon (7½-liter), and finally 2-gallon (10-liter) pot. As the plants begin to grow in earnest, they require liquid feeding with a high-nitrogen fertilizer to ensure they grow at their maximum rate without suffering from any nutrient deficiencies that will slow this growth down.

If the plants are to be planted directly into the soil or a growbag in the greenhouse or tunnel, this can be done at the ½-gallon or 1-gallon (2-liter or 5-liter) stage, as long as the temperatures are suitable. If the structures are heated, this is not a problem, but if the tomatoes are to be grown without heat, they cannot be planted until about the middle of May. I like to grow all our tomatoes so that they are contained in a pot. This means that I can control the type of soil better, as well as prevent infection by soilborne diseases. It is important not to try to rush the plants by overpotting, as this will be detrimental to them due to the excessive amounts of cold and generally wet soil around the roots.

As soon as the plants are ready to be potted into their final 2-gallon (10-liter) container, it is also a good time to consider their eventual method of support. If the tomato plants are to be trained up a bamboo cane, insert this once the plants have been placed into their final position. I like to use strong string to support my tomato plants, and it is therefore important to anchor the string as the plants go into their last pot. My preferred method, and one we have used very successfully at Barnsdale for many years, is simply to lay the string through the inside of the empty pot before potting as normal. The string will be held in place by the weight of the soil, and the tomato plants will have rooted around the string prior to any pressure pulling the string from the weight of the crop. If preferred, the string can also be tied between two of the drainage holes at the bottom of the pot, then pulled up the side of the pot as it is being filled with soil. The string is then cut to the required length, allowing enough to reach and be tied to the top supports.

Once the plants are placed in their final positions, the string is tied to the overhead support. I like to use strong wire for this purpose. As the plants grow, the string is regularly wrapped around the plants, ensuring that it always passes directly over flower clusters and never directly under them, as this may restrict water and nutrient passage to that particular cluster.

As soon as the plants get to about 12 inches (30 cm) tall, they need to be checked at least once a week and any unwanted side shoots removed. These shoots appear in the leaf axil, sapping the plants of vital nutrients, and therefore need to be removed as soon as they are large enough to handle. I prefer to remove them between finger and thumb rather than to use a sharp knife, as it is all too easy to cause damage to the stem of the plant with a knife.

Once the first truss on each plant has set fruit, which is the point at which very small green fruits can be seen, it is time to stop watering with a high-nitrogen feed and feed only with a high-potash liquid fertilizer every ten to fourteen days. Generally I use a seaweed-based liquid feed to promote both the growth and later the flowering and fruiting—although, if I get the chance, I also use homemade liquid feeds made from nettles (for growth) or comfrey leaves (for flowering and fruiting).

As soon as the plants reach six trusses, remove the growing point so that all the plant's efforts are channeled into ripening the fruit already set on the plants. If left to grow on and set more than six trusses, the plant produces fruit that does not reach a usable size or ripen in time.

Each time I enter the hoophouse or greenhouse in which I have tomato plants, I like to tap the supporting wire, which results in the tomato flowers releasing pollen and therefore aiding pollination and increasing ultimate fruit set. This tapping of the wire also causes any whitefly present on the tomato leaves to fly, so any attacks can be spotted at the earliest opportunity and infected leaves removed from the greenhouse. As the fruits on the bottom trusses begin to ripen, the lower, yellowing leaves can be removed. This will not only aid the ripening process, as more light is allowed through to the fruits, but also prevents these leaves from being affected with botrytis (gray mold).

At the end of the growing season, any remaining fruit can be harvested and ripened off the plant. They can be left on the greenhouse benches or on a windowsill, or individually wrapped in paper and placed in a drawer, where they will gradually ripen.

Cucumbers

Cucumbers are expensive to grow, but well worth the effort. They are expensive because they require a minimum nighttime temperature of 68°F (20°C) and minimum daytime temperature of 82°F (28°C) for the duration of the crop. The dependency on temperature means that realistically they require growing in a greenhouse that is heated until the end of May. In the early stages, and until they reach the 2-gallon (10-liter) pot stage, they can be grown using the same method as for tomatoes, except that the seeds are sown directly into a 3-inch (8-cm) pot instead of a seed tray.

Cucumbers are very temperature-dependent and should stay in the greenhouse well into spring.

Due to the different training method, cucumbers are generally tied onto bamboo canes or directly to horizontal supporting wires. As it grows, the main stem can be taken vertically and tied to the supports as it continues growing. The first three side shoots that appear in the axils of the three bottom leaves are removed. If left in place, as fruits are produced on these, they will touch the ground or benches, causing potential botrytis problems. If the fruits are supported off the ground or benches by placing them on upturned pots, it is possible to cut these shoots back to one leaf. The next three side shoots are cut back to the first leaf, with all the remaining shoots cut back to two leaves.

Using this method ensures that a balanced crop of well-sized fruits is produced, without overloading the plant. It is advisable to grow all female varieties of cucumber, as they do not need to be pollinated. If any male flowers do appear on the varieties being grown, they must be removed, as it is the female flowers that produce the cucumbers for harvest. As the crop develops, it may become necessary to tie in some of the side shoots to support the crop and prevent the shoots from breaking under the weight.

Melons

Melons can be treated in the same way as cucumbers for germination, potting, and even growing supports. They are not as expensive a crop as cucumbers to produce, requiring a growing temperature of only 55°F–61°F (13°C–16°C), although some varieties are tolerant of even lower temperatures. Once the plants have produced their second true leaf, remove the growing tip to encourage two further shoots to be produced. These are tied into the supporting wires as they grow until they reach five leaves, at which point the growing tip is removed. This channels all the plant's energy into producing fruit, which appear on the lateral shoots that grow from the two main side shoots.

Melons produce male and female flowers, so it is vital that the greenhouse is ventilated as they begin to flower, to allow insects into the greenhouse for pollination. It is easy to differentiate between the male and female flowers, as the female has a swelling directly behind the flower that becomes the fruit after fertilization. Encourage flowering and fruiting by starting to feed the plants with a high-potash feed as soon as the first flower buds appear. When the first fruit starts to form, thin the tips of each lateral at two leaves beyond this fruit, as for cucumbers.

You will need to support the fruits as they begin to swell, to ensure that they do not snap from the laterals. The best way to do this is with a netted cradle tied to the wire or cane framework. If netting is not available, an old clean pair of tights will do just as good a job.

Each melon plant will sustain a crop of up to five fruits. If, by midsummer, they are looking a bit tired, they can be boosted with a general-purpose liquid feed applied at weekly intervals.

Peppers

Peppers are a crop that is slow to get going, so it is best to sow in February into a heated greenhouse, or in March if the greenhouse is unheated. They need a regular temperature of 60°F–64°F (16°C–18°C) and will quickly suffer at lower temperatures or if in cold, wet soil. Therefore, never overpot peppers or overwater plants. They can be sown and transplanted as for tomatoes, but will suffice in either a ½-gallon (3-liter) or 1-gallon (5-liter) pot, depending on the vigor of the variety being grown. Be aware that the pepper plants will start to suffer if the greenhouse temperature reaches 86°F (30°C), so ventilation in the summer is very important.

The plants should branch into a compact bush without any assistance, but if they do not, then just thin the tips as necessary. Some varieties produce very large peppers, with others producing such an abundant crop that the branches may break under the strain, so keep checking the plants and support where necessary. Pushing a small bamboo cane into the pot and tying the laden branch to this should do the trick.

Eggplant (Aubergines)

Eggplants (aubergines) can be grown using the same method as for peppers, although it is unlikely they will require to be potted into anything larger than a ½-gallon (3-liter) pot.

Container Gardening

It always seems to be assumed that growing fruit, vegetables, and herbs in containers is limited to gardeners who have no garden or other area in which to grow vegetables in the ground. This should not be the case. Fruit, vegetables, and herbs are grown in containers for a variety of reasons, with some being driven by necessity, while others are aesthetic, and some purely for control. It is a method that is available for use by every gardener.

The most obvious and primary reason for growing fruit, vegetables, and herbs in containers is because there is nowhere else for the crops to grow. It could be that there is no garden area—if you live in an apartment, for example—or that within an existing garden there is no room to grow vegetables.

Although unbelievable to some people, most fruit, vegetables, and herbs can be quite beautiful, and there is no reason why they cannot be used primarily as decorative containers that have the added bonus of producing a crop. There is also the controlling aspect of containers. Jerusalem artichoke, for example, is a rampant spreader in the soil. If grown in a container, it can be both contained and controlled. I also use containers to protect crops and have been known to plant climbing French beans, green (runner) beans, outdoor cucumbers, or summer squash (marrows) in half an old copper hot-water tank and allow them to climb up aluminium twirly supports. When the copper has aged, the whole thing looks unusual but very pleasing to the eye, and it has the added benefit of preventing any slug or snail damage to the plants because this pest will not travel over copper.

When it comes to types of container that can be used, there are a couple of basic requirements. The main one is that the container has adequate drainage holes so that the soil does not become waterlogged, resulting in the crops rotting. Secondly, it has to be small enough or large enough to do the job required of it. What the container is made of or looks like is not desperately relevant. If you don't like the look of potatoes grown in a stack of old car tires, painted or not, then don't use them—it really is as simple as that.

We have used various containers in the past to grow fruit, vegetables, and herbs, ranging from handmade (and plastic imitation) terra-cotta pots, to black plastic pots, to homemade containers, to old sinks—and even a pair of our head gardener's old boots!

Container gardening can be useful in any garden, not just those with limited space.

The soil never became waterlogged because all of these containers had enough holes in them that all excess water could easily drain out. The use of *crocks* is very important, as it prevents the drainage holes from becoming blocked, which would cause the container to become too wet. The classic crock is a broken piece of terra-cotta pot that sits nicely over a large drainage hole, but you can use stones or even a layer of coarse gravel as long as the materials do not interfere with the passage of water out of the pot.

Choosing Your Potting Mix

Once you've decided on the type of container and put the crocks in place, the next step is to choose potting mix and fill the container with it. When you are selecting potting mix, choose bags that are not faded or worn—the older the bag, the longer the potting mix will have sat around, releasing its nutrients. In this case, the mix will come with no available fertilizer, and that's a big part of what you're paying for. What you also need to consider, however, is that this fertilizer may be put into the soil at too high a rate, which will mean that plants sown or potted into it may be scorched off. Always buy potting mix that looks as if it has just been delivered.

Making Your Own Containers

COIR HYPERTUFA MIX
- Two parts coir
- One part coarse sand
- One part fresh cement
- Yellow cement dye

OTHER MATERIALS
- Two strong cardboard boxes
- Chicken wire
- Bamboo canes
- Wire cutters
- Pliers
- Wire brush

These containers are easy to make because they are molded around an existing pot (or a cardboard box, if making a trough). Due to its makeup, the tufa will need some strengthening. I always use pieces of chicken wire sandwiched in the center as extra support. The principles for making both pots and troughs are the same, so in this instance I will use making a trough as an example.

1. Find two boxes that fit into each other so that there is about a 2-inch (5-cm) gap between the two, around the edges. The inner box needs to be of the size that you would require the internal dimensions of the container to be. Place the outer cardboard box on the floor in an area out of the way, but also frost-free if this operation is being carried out in the winter.

2. Mix the hypertufa and put a 1-inch (2½-cm) layer in the bottom of the box. I like to preform my strengthening wire (rabbit fencing) into the required shape, which is exactly the same as the boxes, only 1 inch (2 ½ cm) smaller than the outer box and 1 inch (2 ½ cm) larger than the inner one, so that it sits exactly between the two. It is also quite feasible simply to cut the wire into sheets the same size as the bottom and each of the sides. Bear in mind that the top edges of the wire need to be 1 inch (2½ cm) lower than the top of the finished container.

3. At this point it is worth thinking about drainage, so cut about six 2-inch (5-cm) pieces of bamboo cane taken from the thick ends on the canes. Push them into the mix so that they are evenly spaced, until they hit the bottom of the cardboard box, which should leave about 1 inch ($2\frac{1}{2}$ cm) sticking up.

   The next 1-inch ($2\frac{1}{2}$-cm) layer of mix is then placed onto the wire base and leveled to the top of the bamboo canes. It is important to firm the mix well to eliminate any air pockets that would weaken the container when it is dry.

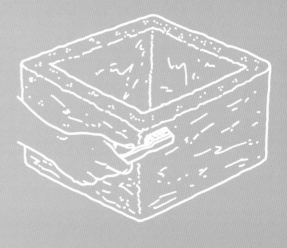

Create drainage holes with evenly spaced pieces of bamboo cane.

4. The next stage is to place the inner box in position, on top of the finished base and in the center of the outer box so that the gap around it is even.

5. It is now time to force the mix in between the two boxes, ensuring that the wire support is sandwiched in the center. It is again important to firm the mix well to eliminate air pockets, but be careful not to also force the cardboard boxes so that your container becomes misshapen. Placing bricks inside the inner box helps to overcome this problem, ensuring that the internal dimensions remain as required. As far as the outside of the container is concerned, a slightly uneven look to the trough seems very pleasing to the eye and not so "manufactured." Leave for at least 48 hours to dry fully before removing the internal and external boxes. The canes are also pushed out at this stage, leaving nicely sized and ample drainage for the container.

6. The final task is to remove the glossy areas where the hypertufa mix was in contact with the cardboard, making the container look older and not so new. This can be easily achieved by giving the outside of the trough or pot a light brushing with a wire brush. Do not get too carried away, otherwise the supporting wire may become visible. I also find that rounding the edges slightly gives the finished product a much nicer appearance.

Container gardening is a very popular method for growing herbs.

The type of general-purpose organic potting mix that you use is not crucial, but we have used peat-free mix at Barnsdale to grow our containerized fruit, vegetables, and herbs since the 1990s and have found it to be excellent. For shorter- and medium-term crops, such as lettuce, radishes, scallions, carrots, multi-sown beets (beetroot), tomatoes, melons, new potatoes, and so on, you can simply use a proprietary mix straight out of the bag. If growing longer-term crops, such as brassicas, it is beneficial to add a proportion of soil to the mix because they like a firm and "meaty" soil in which to grow. A mixture of equal parts soil, proprietary potting mix, and compost is ideal, although this may make moving the container difficult, due to the weight of the soil. Still, once the containers are in position, you shouldn't need to move them.

Watering and Supplementary Feeding

The only problem with growing crops in containers is that they require constant monitoring for water and supplementary feeding. Being out of the ground, a container is more exposed to the drying elements (sun and wind), so will invariably dry much quicker than crops grown in the ground. The side effect of this will either be crops that bolt readily or ones, such as root crops, that become woody.

During the spring and summer at Barnsdale, we check the productive containers at least three times a day—that is, not necessarily watered three times a day, but checked to see if they need water. For our brassicas in containers, we use our three-part mix is to maximize the water-holding capacity of the container. This is because the organic-matter constituent, compost, has an excellent capacity to retain moisture, very much more so than soil and bagged potting mix. If it is not possible to check containers for water this regularly, a watering system really is the answer. This can range from a timer-controlled system that operates from an electrical supply through various degrees of complexity right down to ones that are just a water-filled bag with a tube that goes from the bag down into the container.

All soil bought from a garden center or DIY store will have a proportion of fertilizer in it, but not a great deal, so supplementary feeding will be required to maximize crop production and ultimate harvest. The organic feed used will depend on the crop grown, although the simple rule is to apply a fertilizer high in nitrogen (N) to stimulate crop growth, whereas a fertilizer high in potash is used to maximize the production of flowers and subsequent fruits. These are easily applied when watering, as most come in liquid form or are water-soluble. Each product will list the amount to be added to water and how often to apply, although this is usually every ten to fourteen days.

It is worth bearing in mind that the soil contained in the container can be used in exactly the same way as the soil in the ground: once one crop has been harvested, you can use the same soil for the following crop. You may have to top it up, depending on the amount of root on the crop, but any subsequent crops will require immediate feeding because there will be no fertilizer in the potting mix, as opposed to when you first purchased it.

Reusing Containers

At the end of each growing season, you need to empty the container and either spread its contents on the garden or put it on the compost heap. Unless the contents of the container are primarily soil-based, it is best to replace it each year. Soil-based potting mixes can be used again, but not for the same crop because there may be a risk of pest or disease buildup like there would be for crops grown in the ground. If you replace the contents of containers annually, you won't need to worry about crop rotation and what crops you will grow in each container because there will be fresh potting mix each year and, thus, no chance of pests and diseases building up.

Using Supports

The perfect way to gain more space in a productive garden is to grow plants upward. In this way, the only area taken up by the plant is that into which it is planted. There are, of course, the obvious climbing vegetables, such as green (runner) beans, climbing French beans, outdoor cucumbers, and peas, and the less obvious ones such as zucchini (courgettes), spaghetti squash, gherkins, and a wide range of other squashes. To go along with the wide range of vegetables that you can train upward is a wide range of supports that you can use.

Walls and Fences

Probably the easiest and most obvious structure on which to grow the productive crops mentioned is a wall or fence. In order for this to be suitable, it must be south- or west-facing, so that the vegetables will gain enough sunlight to be as productive as possible. These vegetables are annuals and do not hold themselves to walls or fences, so they would need supports on which to cling. I like to use a strong galvanized wire running horizontally across all the fences here at Barnsdale as a matter of course; if growing beans on a fence, to these wires I add much thinner vertical wires. The main horizontal wires are spaced 12 inches (30 cm) apart, and the thinner vertical wire uses the same spacing so that squares are formed.

If preferred, garden twine can be used instead of the vertical wire. At each point of contact, the vertical wire is wrapped around the stronger horizontal wire so that it is the stronger wires that take the strain from the weight of crop. The vertical wires are in place for the beans to twine around as they climb upward because the horizontal wires are just too far apart for this purpose. The bean shoots may need gentle persuasion to direct them in the desired direction to prevent clogging of shoots on one or two of the vertical wires. If training zucchini (courgettes), spaghetti squash, gherkins, or other squashes, tie onto the horizontal wires as soon as they are long enough. As these are not twining vegetables, they do not necessarily require the vertical wires for growing upward. The wires must be firmly attached so that they can cope with the weight of the crop. In years when climbing vegetables are not grown against these wall or fences, due to the crop rotation, annual flowering plants can be grown instead.

The other method of training climbing vegetables on a wall or fence is to use a trellis. It needs to be permanently attached with strong screws or nails to prevent the weight of the crop from pulling it off. As with the wires, bean shoots may need to be gently directed to ensure a good, even coverage of the trellis, while non-twining plants can be tied regularly. When using garden twine to tie in these very delicate shoots, ensure that it is soft in nature and not coarse because, if the string rubs on the shoot, the coarse twine may cause irreversible damage to the shoot.

Bamboo canes are often used to support climbing beans.

Tepees and Obelisks

Tepees or obelisks can be used to great effect out in the productive garden, or in among flowering plants in the general borders. Green (runner) and climbing French beans are traditionally grown up long bamboo canes pushed into the ground as an upturned "V" and connected together by a cane ridge. Although very effective, this method does require a reasonably large area, whereas individual tepees or obelisks do not.

I find both types of climbing bean very ornamental when in flower, and try to use them in the flower borders to give color most of the summer, up to a height of 6 feet (a little less than 2 m). In order to get the shoots long enough to carry a big enough crop of beans, 8-foot (about 2½-m) bamboo canes must be used to make your tepee. Push these about 12 inches (30 cm) into the ground, at about a 75-degree angle, with 12–18

Bean Trench

The only real problem with green (runner) beans is that they can become stringy and inedible. There are two reasons for this: either they are too old (green beans are always better when picked young and fresh) or the plants have been allowed to become too dry. Both problems are easily avoided by picking regularly and also ensuring that there is always moisture at the roots of the plants.

The best way to keep green (runner) beans moist throughout the summer is to grow them over a bean trench. It is a simple method that involves digging a 36-inch- (90-cm)-wide trench in the place the crop will be grown. The length of the trench depends on what is required to accommodate the green (runner) beans. The depth of the trench needs only to be that of a spade, about 9 inches (23 cm), with the soil piled along one edge. The bottom of the trench is then filled with organic matter that would usually be destined for the compost bin, such as brussels-sprout leaves and shredded newspaper, as well as other moisture-retaining materials such as well-rotted horse manure. The idea is to half-fill the trench, if possible, with all this type of material because it rots down to good organic matter that helps to conserve moisture in the bottom half of the trench and in the area feeding the green (runner) bean roots.

It is prudent to have a contingency plan in place in case of a very long and hot summer, so that water can be applied to the plants if the bean trench cannot cope. I like to use water that has been recycled from roofs and stored in a rain barrel. After I have erected the tepee supports over the trench to be used for the beans, I run a length of soaker hose along the inside edge of each row of canes. It needs to be just buried under the soil surface so that water evaporation is kept to a minimum. Each end of the soaker hose is connected to a "T" piece, then one pipe runs to the rain barrel. It can run from this very low pressure because the water leaks out of the pipes, which are made from recycled rubber car tires, as small droplets. When using this system, it is very easy to forget what stringy green beans are like.

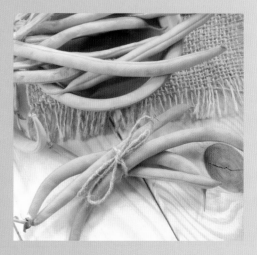

inches (30–45 cm) of space between each of the canes. About 12 inches (30 cm) from the top of the canes, bunch together and tie using garden twine. Rather than growing the beans straight up the canes, you could train them so that they wrap around the outside, potentially giving a greater length of shoot and therefore a heavier crop.

Homemade or bought obelisks are very ornamental and can be used again in the productive areas or in the flower borders. The beans can be trained in the same way as for a tepee, or used as a companion to a permanent climber already being grown on the obelisk. I often put both green (runner) and climbing French beans on obelisks that have either roses or clematis already growing up them. The bean flowers add enormously to the ornamental garden and, as a bonus, they produce crops, too.

Pergolas

I also like to use pergolas as supports for growing climbing vegetables and, although long bamboo canes can be pushed into the ground and tied to the top of the pergola at 24-inch (60-cm) intervals, I find these somewhat obtrusive. Instead I prefer to use soft but strong string that can be tied to the top of the pergola, then held in the ground with a homemade wire stake. Using the string means that it is the plants that are seen, in all their glory, and not their supports. In the case of the non-twining plants, wrap the string around the growing tips of the plants to hold them in position.

"Pea Sticks"

The majority of peas are not self-supporting, and even with those that are, you'd still invariably have to use supports on windy sites. The use of twiggy "pea sticks" is a practice that has been carried out very successfully over many years. There is usually no need to buy pea sticks; you can use long, twiggy branches—24–36 inches (60–90 cm)

long—from any tree. I keep suitable branches that have been cut from ornamental as well as fruiting trees during the winter, unless they have been removed due to pest or disease.

Due to the tendrils pea plants have in each leaf joint, which will twine around and grip onto almost anything, fancy supports are not required. Once the peas have been planted outside and any cloche covering has been removed, the sticks can be inserted into the ground either side of the row of peas. They are pushed into the ground at a slight angle, so that the twiggy tops meet over the row of peas, giving the plants ample support. As the peas grow, they will grip onto the twigs for support with no assistance from you.

Tree Trunks

The final technique I have used to support climbing vegetables is by making use of the trunk of a tree which had lost its top half in very windy weather. The vegetable plants were able to hold themselves up by making use of the strong but thin wire I had attached vertically to the tree. The beans were left to scramble in whatever direction they wanted to go, while all the other climbers had to be tied onto the wires. It was particularly successful with gherkins; by the end of the season, the trunk of the tree was invisible, being totally covered by this rampant vegetable.

There are inevitably going to be many different materials that can be used as supports that I have not mentioned, but basically anything that is able to support a crop in an upward direction will fit the bill.

Chapter 4

Caring for Your Crops

Controlling Weeds

All weeds in the productive area are a problem. Not only do they use vital water required by the crops, but they remove essential nutrients from the soil as well. If left unchecked, weeds will cause a reduced harvest for these reasons. In addition, with vegetables and herbs they may smother crops, at best preventing them from growing or at worst killing them completely.

One of the best ways of eliminating weeds from a productive area before crops are grown is to use the stale seedbed method described on page 37. The easiest way to control weeds in orchards of apples, pears, cherries, or plums is to cover the bare soil with grass. This may prevent a small amount of water and nutrients from being available to the trees, but for the amateur gardener it has a minimal effect on the subsequent crops and makes controlling weeds much easier. The reason it is excellent as weed control is because the grass will need to be regularly mowed, which not only cuts the tops of the grass blades but also cuts down any weeds. The competition from the grass also makes it harder for weeds to get a firm hold.

This method is not really feasible in vegetable, herb, and soft fruit areas because the crops will not remain in exactly the same places each year. There are four basic methods of weed control in this situation: mulching, hoeing, closer plant spacing, and green manures. Mulching in the vegetable areas has to be short term because even the longest crops will generally not be in the ground for more than eight to nine months. You should therefore look to use materials that can be dug into the soil as a soil improver once the crop has been harvested, so compost, green compost, well-rotted horse or cow manure, grass clippings, and cardboard can all be used. The permanent or longer term herb and soft fruit crops can be mulched with the full range of mulches (see page 148).

If mulching is not an option, hoeing between the crops works well, but can be quite hard work. Draw hoes, Dutch hoes, onion hoes, or wheeled hoes can be used, with the latter only suitable for crops grown in rows. Once the weeds have been hoed off, they are left on the soil surface to dry out before being taken to the compost bin. Remember to hoe walking backward, so that you do not replant the hoed weeds with your feet by pushing them back into the soil.

When using the bed system, weeds are kept at bay by planting the crops closer together so that they cover the ground better. This inhibits water and vital light getting to the weed seed, preventing them from germinating and growing. The closer spacing also helps to minimize water evaporation from the soil surface.

Hoeing between rows is hard, but effective, work.

Finally, green manures can be successfully used in vacant parts of the productive areas to minimize weed growth, by occupying the ground themselves as they grow. At the end of the life of the green manure, chop it down to ground level, allow it to wilt, and dig into the soil, complete with any weeds present. If using a non-nitrogen-fixing green manure, it will be in the ground for such a short length of time that any weeds that do grow will not have time to seed.

Earthing Up Potatoes and Other Vegetables

Earthing up (or hilling) is a process that is used on a wide range of crops for varying reasons. It involves the pulling of soil onto the crop, or part of the crop, in order to carry out the job required. Earthing up a crop is not usually a one-off job where a lot of soil is moved, but rather is carried out three or four times through the growing season, moving a little soil each time. Generally the soil can be earthed up around a crop using either a draw hoe or a spade. I find that earthing up while hoeing between a crop is the easiest and quickest method.

In earthing up potatoes, the edible parts of the plants are kept covered.

Most gardeners will have seen potatoes being grown with a mound or ridge of soil over each row. This process is used not only for potatoes but also for Jerusalem artichokes. The problem with both of these crops is that many of their tubers—the parts we eat—are produced close to the soil surface. Although this makes harvesting easier, if

the tubers are exposed to the light, they become green and inedible. The first stage of earthing up begins directly after planting, when the classic soil ridge is drawn up over the row of potato tubers just planted. As the crop develops, soil is pulled over the area in which the tubers are being produced to keep them covered and in the dark, so that they can be eaten once they are harvested. We usually start to draw soil over the potato tops when they have reached about 12 inches (30 cm) in height, leaving about 2 inches (5 cm) of tops showing. As the crop develops, we may draw smaller quantities of soil up the ridges just to ensure no potatoes are visible.

Carrots are a crop that can suffer from green shoulder, where the top part of the root is pushed out of the soil and is therefore exposed to the light, which turns green and inedible. The simple cure is to draw soil over the root tops on a regular basis during their growing period. Other crops where the edible part is the stem need to be blanched in order to produce the strength of flavor required. The method for blanching both celery and leeks is to draw soil over the stems to eliminate the light. This lack of light turns celery stems more yellow, while the blanched section of leeks becomes white. To lengthen the edible parts, use the same method as for potatoes, where soil is drawn up the stems while hoeing.

Earthing up can also be used to support a crop. Brassicas, for example, generally like to be very well firmed on planting, but some of the taller and larger-headed crops will require supplementary support. Brussels sprouts, broccoli, cauliflower, and cabbage all benefit from earthing up. As the crop develops and they get to the stage where they may fall over, either due to height or weight of head, draw up the soil from the surrounding area, positioning it around the base of the stem and firming in well. This helps to support the stem and prevents the plant from falling over.

Blanching and Forcing

T he technique of blanching some vegetable varieties has been used for many years as a means of improving the flavor. It involves eliminating the light to all or part of the produce. Some vegetables, such as celery, endive, and chicory, can be somewhat acidic if grown without blanching, while others, such as leeks, have their strong flavor dulled when blanched, making them much more palatable. Other varieties, including Swiss chard (spinach beet) and rhubarb, can be forced. Forcing is a way of getting a young and tender harvest before the outdoor crop is ready, or while the edible part of the crop is tough to eat.

There are several ways in which to blanch crops, with all being simple to carry out—although some are harder work than others.

Celery

There are two distinct types of celery, self-blanching and trench celery, and each has different blanching procedures. When growing self-blanching celery, grow the plants at a closer spacing so that the leaves are almost touching—it is these leaves that create the shade to blanch the stems. I find that most varieties will still hold too much acidity for my palate, so I always give them an extra treatment, which will give them the same yellow stems as are obtained with trench celery but without the hard work. Once the stems have reached the length required, tie a sheet of newspaper around each plant,

enclosing all the stems from the soil up to the leaves. This eliminates all the light and blanches the stems, giving them a much sweeter taste.

These yellow stems are the aim with trench celery, where a trench 8 inches (20 cm) deep and 18 inches (45 cm) wide is dug out and well-rotted manure dug into the bottom. Plant the cell (plug)-raised celery plants into the bottom of this trench in a straight line right down the center.

As the celery plants grow, gradually fill the trench back in so that, at any given time, only the leaves at the tops of the plants are showing. Continue this practice right through the growing season until the trench is filled back to its original level by the surrounding soil. This process ensures the stems of trench celery never see the light and therefore are always well blanched with minimum acidity. One stumbling block I find with this method is that soil falls between the stems as you fill the trench, causing problems when the celery is harvested and taken into the kitchen. This is why I also wrap the clumps of stems in newspaper each time the trench needs to be filled. It makes no difference to the blanching process but does keep the edible stems very clean.

Endive

As trends in foods change, certain vegetables that have been good staple winter produce for many years suddenly become fashionable, but gardeners can be put off growing them because they are unaware of the best methods. Endive is a wonderful hardy winter lettuce that has a firm texture and quite a sharply flavored leaf. Some gardeners enjoy the bitterness of endive, but I prefer them to be sweeter, so I always blanch them before harvesting.

There are two quite simple techniques involved that need to be implemented, usually three to four weeks prior to harvesting. As they are grown on the soil surface, the plants can simply be covered with a flower pot to exclude the light. Make sure the holes at the bottom of the pot are taped over so that the plants are in complete darkness or they will not blanch properly. The problem with using pots on a windy site is that they invariably blow away, so if this method is not practical you can blanch the endive by tying the leaves up with string. Pull string around the outside leaves, then tighten; the hearts of the plants will blanch and become yellow, while the very outer leaves remain green and bitter. If shredded before eating, a small amount of these greener and bitter leaves adds variety to a salad.

Chicory

Another good winter salad crop is chicory. You really need to enjoy eating chicory, as it takes quite a lot of work before the leaves are ready for harvest. The top growth, or *chicons*, of witloof chicory can be harvested from November to March from a June or July sowing. In the autumn, lift the roots that will be used for forcing. Trim the top leaves to within ½ inch (1 cm) of the root and lay them in a box of moist soil or sand. Keep the box in a cool place until it is needed for forcing.

To keep up a good continuity of chicons, it is necessary to plunge roots for forcing every three to four weeks. Use a deep container that is filled with moist garden soil or peat substitute. Plunge the roots into this, ensuring that they are firmed well. Cover the roots with another 9 inches (23 cm) of soil or peat substitute, again firm well and put a lid on the top to block out all the light. Leave the box in a warm, dark place for the chicons to be produced.

After about four to five weeks, the chicons will have grown about 6–8 inches (15–20 cm) and will be ready for harvest. Lift out the complete root and cut the top growth away from the roots, about ½ inch (1 cm) from the top of the root. These roots can then be used to force another crop before they are discarded.

Leeks

I think leeks are one of the great winter vegetables. It is important in any vegetable garden to have something that breaks the monopoly held by the brassica family throughout the winter. When grown as a multi-sown crop, leeks are harvested when about the size of scallions (spring onions), at a time when they are young, juicy, and tender. As they are picked at such an early stage, they have a good flavor, but not one that is overpowering. There is therefore no necessity to calm any strong flavors by blanching.

This is not the case with main-crop leeks, however, as the very strong leek flavors are produced in the green leaves. To mute the flavor, leeks are blanched so that as much white stem (which contains the more subtle leek flavors) is produced as possible. As with all blanching methods, the stems of leeks will turn white when light is excluded, and the easiest way to do this is by using the soil into which they are planted. I like to plant my leeks either into dibbled holes or at the bottom of a trench. When planting into holes, raise the leeks in a seedbed, in very much the same way as you would brassicas. When the seedlings reach about 8 inches (20 cm) in height, they are ready for transplanting into their final positions. Using a dibble, make a hole about 6 inches (15 cm) deep, with the distance apart being dependent on the variety being grown. Trim the roots of each plant by about two-thirds and the leaves by about half, before dropping them into the hole roots-first.

Trimming the roots encourages the leeks to root faster than if they were untrimmed, while the leaf height is reduced to balance the fact that you have just cut off most of the roots. At this stage it is not important to refill the hole, as this may inhibit the growth of the leeks; instead fill the hole with water from a watering can, which will draw down enough soil to cover the roots and get the plants growing. The leeks grow and fill the hole before expanding out into the surrounding soil. Once the leeks are more than 6 inches (15 cm) above ground level, I start drawing soil over these stems to lengthen the white part of the stem, and as they grow I continue to draw soil up.

Traditionally, leeks are grown in a trench, using very much the same system as for celery. If using this method, it is beneficial to wrap the stems if soil is finding its way between the leaves. When growing show leeks, plant them at ground level and blanch the very large stems using newspaper or cardboard.

Rhubarb, Sea Kale, and Swiss Chard (Spinach Beet)

Excluding the light from crops not only moderates the sharp or strong flavor of some crops, it can also force plants to generate a crop when they would not usually be productive. This method of forcing crops can be successfully used on rhubarb, sea kale, and Swiss chard (spinach beet), which can produce a very early spring crop of tender and sweet stems.

It is possible to force rhubarb so that you get an early crop of light pink, deliciously sweet stems that contain no acidity whatsoever. The method is simple, but first there has to be more than one clump of rhubarb to force successfully each year. This is because the process of forcing does weaken the clump to a certain degree, and rhubarb seems to like a two-year rest before being forced again, so three clumps in the garden is important to complete the annual rotation. Each autumn, lift one of the clumps once cold, frosty weather has been forecast, and leave it on the soil surface for two to three weeks. This exposure to freezing weather will encourage the clump to produce much earlier growth in the spring. Once it has been well and truly frosted, replant the clump and cover it with a forcing jar, bucket, or large pot.

It is important to exclude all light, so ensure that all the holes in the pot are taped up. The stems will grow to be very spindly in appearance, with the small leaves being completely yellow, due to the complete lack of light. Once the stems are long enough, harvest them and replace the cover to get one more crop.

It is possible to obtain two crops before the main clumps begin to produce, but do not be tempted to harvest more than this, as a clump will struggle to recover from a third forcing in one year. In the second year, move on to one of the other clumps, leaving the clump that was forced first to produce its edible stems in a completely natural way.

The same method can be used to harvest early crops of both Swiss chard (spinach beet) and sea kale, with the latter being a permanent crop that can be forced every year, so it is not necessary to have lots of clumps around the garden. As for Swiss chard (spinach beet), this is a hardy annual crop that can be forced to produce two good crops of tender stems prior to the crop being lifted as the new plants become ready for harvest in summer. Both will force successfully without being lifted and frosted.

Protecting Your Crops

An obvious and easy method of preventing damage to crops by pests is to ensure the crop is not at a susceptible stage when the pest is prevalent. Most pests will attack the young and tender parts of plants, so ensure these have matured and are therefore not so tasty to the pests by planning the sowing and planting times around the pest's life cycle.

This can be easily demonstrated with carrots, which are particularly susceptible to the carrot fly when the roots are young and tender. The carrot fly lays its eggs in the

Carrot plants are protected from carrot fly under an enviromesh cover.

soil next to the developing roots, with the emerging larvae burrowing into the roots before emerging as adults. There can be up to three life cycles per year, but it is the first, at the end of May or early June, that seems to cause the worst damage. The carrot flies are attracted by the smell of the young carrots, with the larvae finding it easier to burrow into the softer, tender flesh than that of more mature roots. You should therefore time the sowing of carrots so that they are more mature by the period that the carrot flies are active or so that they germinate and grow after the life cycle has been completed. As the flies are attracted by smell, it is also prudent not to thin carrots at this time of year. The process of thinning releases a strong odor that will only attract the carrot fly to your crop.

We can prevent pests from reaching our crops by either placing a physical barrier in their way or controlling them by using predators. If predators are being used to control any pests present, this is exactly what they will do: control them, but never completely eradicate the pest. The purpose is to keep the pest under control so that it does not cause too much damage. The reason the predator will never completely eradicate the pest is that, if it did, it would have nothing to feed on. The only way to keep crops completely pest- and disease-free is to place a physical barrier in their way. As will be seen, some of the techniques used involve everyday materials, while others require purchasing, but all methods are cheap and easy to employ.

Physical Barriers
Row Cover

Row cover, also called garden fabric, is a woven material used primarily to protect crops against frost, but it also creates an excellent barrier against flying pests. If you plan to use the fabric to protect a crop against subzero temperatures, it needs to lie directly on the crop because the air trapped between the fibers is what provides insulation. If you plan to use the fabric for crop protection against flying pests, however, the fabric needs to be above the crop but not necessarily directly on top of the plants.

This material is ideal for protection against the carrot root fly. You can place it over the crop on sowing or planting and leave it in place until either the flies have completed their first life cycle or the crop becomes large enough not to be troubled by the carrot fly.

When held in place properly, plastic covering over a tunnel creates an impenetrable barrier to flying pests.

This fantastic material is light-, water-, and air-permeable, so you can leave it on or over a crop (the only problem is the chance of slight leaf scorch on sunny days where the fabric touches the crop). Although garden fabric is permeable to all of the important elements that a crop requires to grow successfully and without hindrance, it provides a completely impenetrable barrier to all flying pests if attached to the ground correctly.

Enviromesh

Enviromesh is another material that lies over the crop to keep all flying pests from getting to and damaging the produce beneath. It is made from plastic and consists of thousands of tiny square holes that are small enough to allow the easy passage of water and air but not pests. The material is light and easy to move, and it can lie on any structure placed over the crop.

Enviromesh is pliable and long-lasting; it will continue to protect against pests for many growing seasons as long as the edges are sealed to the ground.

Cloches

The term *cloche* can refer to coverings, such as glass bell jars, used to cover individual plants, or it can refer to larger coverings, such as plastic-covered tunnels, over multiple plants or even entire gardens; the latter type is described here. Cloches can be covered with various materials, depending on their desired function. Gardeners often use plastic-covered cloches over early crops that require protection from the weather. If the plastic is held down in a way that prevents pests from getting underneath it, it will both provide a barrier that flying pests cannot penetrate and protect the crop from the cold weather.

If you are erecting a cloche over a crop strictly for the purpose of protecting that crop from pests, plastic may not be the best covering material, particularly as the season extends and the weather warms. With the buildup of potentially damaging heat under the cloche, the answer is either to ventilate—which creates an obvious entry point for flying pests—or to cover the cloche with a breathable barrier. Either garden fabric or enviromesh will prevent flying pests from attacking the crop while allowing water and air to pass through freely so that the plants will not overheat in hot weather.

Soda-Bottle Cloches

Many of us recycle our plastic soda bottles, but they can also be very handy tools to protect plants from flying insects, birds, slugs, and snails. To make an individual cloche

Individual plastic coverings are similar to the soda-bottle cloche concept.

out of a soda bottle, all you need to do is cut off the bottom of the bottle with scissors and remove the cap. You then set the bottle right-side up over the plant.

If using the bottle for protection against small flying pests, it is advisable to put a piece of netting, old stocking, or something similar over the hole left by the cap and hold it in place with a rubber band. Be sure to use a breathable material to cover the hole so that the plant inside does not overheat.

Once the plant has grown enough to touch the sides of the bottle, remove the bottle and use it elsewhere. It's important to note that, if you are gardening on a windy site, soda-bottle cloches are probably not the best option for protection because the bottles are lightweight and will blow away in a medium-strength wind.

Plastic Netting

We like to use either green or black plastic netting because it is less obtrusive and therefore more pleasing to the eye than other colors. In my experience, netting with ½-inch (1½-cm) square holes is not penetrable by cabbage white butterflies or birds, particularly pigeons, and thus is ideal for covering and protecting brassica crops. Position the netting above the crop so that it is not touching any of the plants. If the netting is allowed to lie on the crop, cabbage white butterflies will be able to lay their eggs through it and onto the brassicas. I usually knock four fence posts into the ground and support the netting with strong twine stretched around all four posts and across diagonally from corner to corner. There is no harm in leaving the netting on for the life of the crop because the large holes will not allow too much shade to be cast over the plants.

Cotton String/Twine

If crops such as brassicas or cherries are plagued by birds, you can stretch cotton string or twine between supporting posts or sticks so that the birds cannot fly through the strings and onto the crop. The problem with this method, though, is that birds can easily become trapped in the string, which can badly injure or even eventually kill them.

Poultry Netting

For any gardener who has experienced the devastating effects of a rabbit in his or her crops, poultry netting (a.k.a. chicken wire) is an absolute must. Rabbits will not only devastate vegetable crops and herbs, but they also will strip the bark from fruit trees. It is important to use netting with 1¼-inch (31-mm) holes and a width

Spots where the leaves touch the netting are vulnerable to cabbage white butterflies.

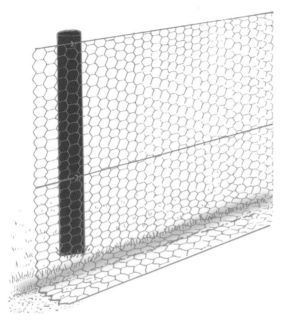

of 48 inches (120 cm). Stretch strong galvanized wire between round fence posts at a height of 36 inches (90 cm). Dig a trench 4 inches (10 cm) deep and 8 inches (20 cm) wide on the outside of the posts to carry the underground part of the netting, placing the soil on the nonproductive side of the trench. Attach the netting to the posts using construction staples and attach the top of the fence to some of the supporting wire using thin galvanized wire. Lay the wire netting across the bottom of the trench and cover with 4 inches (10 cm) of the soil that you removed.

If you follow these instructions to install poultry netting around the entire area to be protected, the crops will be completely safe from attacks by rabbits. When rabbits approach the fence, because it is a barrier, their instinct will be to dig straight down. When they do this, the wire that extends 8 inches (20 cm) will stop them again, and they will hop away. Rabbits will jump over a 36-inch (90-cm)-high fence if they are being chased, but they will not do so when approaching a fence in a normal, stress-free manner.

Galvanized Wire

In a productive garden, deer can be just as devastating as rabbits. Many gardeners who are troubled by deer live in rural areas or areas that border countryside, which means that they also have the potential for rabbit damage. It is therefore necessary to consider deer protection only above the height of the rabbit fencing that is already in place.

Unlike rabbits, deer can jump up to 6 feet (approximately 2 m) high in their normal activity, particularly if there is a juicy crop to be nibbled. To protect against deer, erect 8-foot (2⅖-m) posts to which you can attach the rabbit fencing as well as the galvanized wire used to fend off deer. Knock the posts about 24 inches (60 cm) into the ground, leaving at least 6 feet (approximately 2 m) sticking out of the ground. Stretch three strands of strong galvanized wire above the rabbit fencing and attach it using construction nails at 12-inch (30-cm) intervals up the posts. It will be possible for some larger deer to leap this height, but only when being chased.

Cabbage Root Fly Squares

The material you use to create this barrier can vary depending on what is available at the time. I prefer to make my own squares because they are very easy to construct, and the material is usually free. When considering cabbage root fly protection, my first port of call is the local carpeting store to ask for some free carpet-padding scraps. I can usually get enough to make twenty to thirty squares. Cut the padding into 4-inch (10-cm) squares. With each square, make a cut from one edge into the center and then make two smaller cuts at the top of your first cut (to resemble a "Y"). You then place the cut squares over the plants at ground level to prevent attacks.

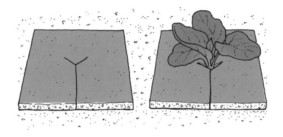

If your young brassica plants are unprotected, cabbage root fly adults land next to them and lay their eggs where the stems meets the soil. After hatching, the larvae burrow down into the soil and feed on the roots of the brassicas, stunting the plants and badly affecting the crop yield. The carpet-padding squares prevent the adults from laying their eggs next to the plant stems, providing an extremely simple barrier against cabbage root fly attack. Once the plants are more mature, you can remove the squares and use them on the next crop of young brassica plants; the carpet-padding squares will last for at least three years. You can use cardboard instead, but it will deteriorate over the season to a point where it disintegrates and thus cannot be reused.

Mole Traps

The only way to deal successfully with a mole problem is to trap the moles. When used correctly, mole traps will execute a quick kill, preventing the moles from suffering. You

set the traps so that they are part of an active tunnel that runs between two molehills. Because moles have a very sensitive sense of smell, you must wear gloves when setting the traps; otherwise, they will detect a foreign smell and not use that particular tunnel.

Hedges

Hedges are very useful against the carrot fly because this pest flies very close to the ground and will not usually fly any higher than 6 inches (15 cm). A dense evergreen hedge that is more than 6 inches (15 cm) high will prevent carrot flies from reaching the young and tasty carrots beyond. An excellent hedge for this purpose is box (*Buxus*), which is also very easy to maintain and looks very formal—incorporating some topiary into the hedge adds an interesting dimension.

Mouse and Rat Traps

There are two types of traps for catching these rodent pests. The humane traps are wire cages that have bait inside. The rodent enters to eat the bait and cannot exit. It can then be released into an area where it will do no harm to the crops. The other type of trap is one that works on a highly tensioned spring that kills the rodent as it attempts to eat the bait. Neither of these rodents is of any benefit in the productive garden, and they can cause a lot of damage to seeds, growing crops, and stored produce.

Scarecrows

People have long used scarecrows to scare birds from freshly sown seed and growing crops. Stationary scarecrows are of no real use because birds quickly realize that they are not angry gardeners ready to kill them and will happily roost on the outstretched arms. Scarecrows that swivel in the wind seem to be much more effective.

Flypaper

Flypaper is a method of controlling flying pests in the greenhouse that works on the "hit-and-miss" principle. The trap consists of a strip of plastic that is coated with a very sticky glue; some flypaper also has a sweet substance to attract the bugs, and some even contain an insecticide. You hang the strips up in the greenhouse, and the pest flies into it, sticks to the glue, and is unable to fly away. Flypaper can also trap some beneficial insects—although it usually catches far more pests. The traps can also be considered excellent pest detectors because regular monitoring of the glue will indicate a pest problem.

Cardboard and Grease

The combination of cardboard, grease, and a small wooden stick (like a tongue depressor) makes another sticky trap that is very effective in trapping flea beetles. The sure signs of attack from this pest on crops such as turnips and radishes are tiny holes in the leaves. These holes cause a reduction in the size of the roots harvested because they reduce the amount of leaf area able to photosynthesize, slowing the plant's growth.

This very simple method involves cutting a rectangular piece of cardboard 4 inches (10 cm) wide and about 6 inches (15 cm) long and coating one side of it with grease. Any grease will do as long as it has a similar consistency to petroleum jelly. When small insects come into contact with the trap, they stick to the grease.

The reflection of light from a compact disc scares birds away from your crops.

To use this type of trap, you hold the stick in one hand and the cardboard in the other. Turn the cardboard so that the grease side is facing down, about 2 inches (5 cm) above the leaves of the crop. Run the stick along the row of plants so that it hits the tops of the leaves, and move the cardboard along with it. Flea beetles jump when disturbed—hence their name—so they will jump straight onto the grease, where they become stuck. Discard the cardboard once you reach the end of the row. All of the flea beetles should be stuck to it and none left on the leaves of the crop.

Pheromone Trap

A pheromone trap is a triangular box that has a sticky card placed on the bottom and is laced with the pheromone of the female codling moth. Gardeners hang these traps among apple and pear trees during mid-May at a ratio of one trap per five trees.

This type of trap works because the female pheromone attracts the male codling moth into the triangular trap, where it then gets stuck on the sticky pad and dies, meaning that it is unable to fertilize the female's eggs, preventing new larvae that would have burrowed into and damaged the fruit crop.

Compact Discs (CDs)

CDs make excellent deterrents to birds. You can hang them on strings from branches in fruit orchards, and you can place them on a stick stuck in the ground at an angle near vegetable crops. It is important that the CDs are able to spin because it is the subsequent reflection of light that scares away the birds.

Grease Band

Adult female winter moths are wingless, and because they overwinter in the soil at the base of apple and pear trees, the most effective method of control is to stop them from climbing these trees to lay their eggs. Becaused they begin to emerge starting in mid-November, you should tie a grease band around each stem and supporting stake of all susceptible trees by the end of October.

You can buy grease bands from garden centers and home stores, but they are very easy to make. Each trap is a 4-inch (10-cm) strip of plastic that circles the tree trunk about 18 inches (45 cm) from the ground and is tied in place with soft string. You coat the plastic with some thick grease so that when the female winter moths try to climb the tree to deposit their eggs, they become stuck in the grease and cannot progress any farther. You will need to use new bands each October.

Peach Umbrella

Many peaches and nectarines seem to suffer from peach leaf curl. Although it is unsightly, it rarely causes the trees too much harm. In a severe attack, however, the tree will drop leaves, which impacts on the final yield of the tree. The spores of this disease are spread by rain, so the best way of controlling it is to keep the rain away from the tree leaves. This is easier on fan-trained specimens than freestanding trees, but you can adapt an umbrella for any type of tree.

An easy but time-consuming method is to attach a sheet of plastic above the fan-trained tree and, every time rain is in the forecast, roll the plastic down to keep the leaves dry; you then roll it up again once the rain has passed. A less labor-intensive method is to construct a semicircular plastic-covered frame above the tree that will act as an umbrella, keeping the majority, if not all, of the rain off the leaves.

Those with expert woodworking skills, however, can construct a frame from 1 x ¾-inch (2½ x 2-cm) lumber as the outer frame and use strong wire for the supporting ribs. Attach the plastic with battens and nails. This structure will last many seasons and is not as obtrusive as a plastic sheet.

Companion Planting

The main problem with physical barriers is that many are not aesthetically pleasing, while using flowers as companion plants definitely adds extra beauty to a productive area. If fruit, vegetables, and herbs are produced in areas that are not close to any ornamental planting, it is important to provide some in order to attract insects that will help with organic pest control. It is worth considering a small area for growing flowers or companion planting among the fruit, vegetables, and herb gardens. Plants such as *Tagetes*, calendulas, poppies, nasturtiums, *Limnanthes*, and many others are very effective in attracting the adults of a wide range of beneficial insects into the productive garden and will also add color and interest.

It is also said that by planting some types of vegetables next to others, it is possible to prevent pest damage to susceptible crops. The classic example of this is with carrots, where the planting of onions or garlic on either side of a row of carrots is supposed to deter carrot flies, as the flies cannot smell the carrots over the powerful smell of onions. It does work, but research has shown that you need to grow at least ten rows of onions or garlic for each row of carrots, so you would really need to like onions!

Poppies are among the plants that attract beneficial insects to the garden.

Naturally Occurring Predators

Companion plants will attract a range of naturally occurring predators, most of which are common to gardens, and it is the larvae of some and the adults of others that will eat the pests. For example, lacewings, hoverflies, and ladybug larvae, as well as wasps and earwigs, eat aphids. Ground beetles, centipedes, frogs, and toads consume slugs and snails.

Birds and bats should also be encouraged into the garden. Place birdhouses in trees because many bird species feed on pests—many small nesting birds are voracious. While raising their brood of chicks, a pair of adult birds can collect between 7,000 and 14,000 caterpillars to feed themselves and their chicks. Now, not all of these caterpillars will be pests, but the majority of them will be, and can you think of a more beautiful way to control cabbage white butterfly caterpillars?

Also place bat boxes in trees; an average bat can consume up to 3,500 insects per night. Again, not all of these insects are bad, but it's likely that the majority of them will be.

Ladybugs require something in which to crawl, so a bundle of canes tied together and hung up is ideal. The canes need to be only 3–4 inches (7½–10 cm) in length and the holes in the center of the canes wide enough for the adult beetles to crawl into. Lacewing adults are just as easy to overwinter. A soda bottle cut in half, filled with rolled-up corrugated cardboard, and then hung up, is ideal.

Frogs and toads require a water source, which may be something as simple as a bucket sunk into the ground, but make sure that there are bricks or something similar in the bottom that will enable the animals to get in and out of the bucket. Ground beetles and centipedes require a leaf, soil, or mulch cover under which to hide.

There is no doubt that attracting wildlife into the garden not only increases the diversity and pleasure of one's productive areas, but also makes the job of pest control much, much easier. Having a population already there at the start of each year will only make growing much more pleasurable.

Hedgehogs

In the United Kingdom, hedgehogs are excellent controllers of slugs and snails, but they need somewhere to shelter if the area's undergrowth is not ample enough. Once a gardener has attracted these natural predators into the garden, it is important for him or her to keep them there, which means overwintering them; hedgehogs require only a pile of sticks or branches under which to hibernate.

Introduced Predators

All of the foregoing naturally occurring predators can be used to control pests on outdoor crops, but for greenhouse and conservatory pests, there is a range of produced predators that will do the job. They come from much warmer climates and thus need to be bred in a controlled environment and introduced into crops on a regular basis.

Aphidius is a tiny black insect that lays its eggs into aphids. When the eggs hatch, the resulting larvae feed on the aphid, killing it. These predators need a regular temperature of 64°F (18°C) to survive and work efficiently.

Encarsia formosa is a small parasitic wasp that looks very much like a miniature hoverfly. It controls whitefly by laying its eggs in the whitefly scales (eggs), which then turn black. The resulting larvae eat the contents of the scales before they develop. *Encarsia formosa* requires a temperature of 61°F–68°F (16°C–20°C).

Phytoseuilius persimilis, just like its prey, is a small mite. It devours red spider mites by crawling from leaf to leaf. Because it can only crawl, the leaves of the crop must be touching for it to cover a wide enough range. To work properly, *Phytoseuilius persimilis* also requires a temperature of 61°F–68°F (16°C–20°C).

Cryptolaemus beetles are relatives of the ladybug, with both the adults and larvae feeding on mealybug eggs and nymphs. The adults lay their eggs directly into the eggs of the mealybugs. They require an average temperature of 68°F (20°C) to work well.

Nemasys is a microscopic nematode that comes dehydrated in a packet and is brought back to life by adding water. There are three types of nematodes that each work on either vine weevil, daddy longlegs larvae, or chafer grubs. They require a constant soil temperature of no lower than about 41°F (5°C) to work.

Nemaslug is also a microscopic nematode that kills slugs and snails. It requires the same minimum temperature as Nemasys to work, which means that it is usually effective from April to September.

As you can see by the required temperatures, only the latter two predators can be used outside. All of these predators need to be reintroduced on a regular basis in order to keep any pests under control.

Using Organic Sprays

There are only a small number of pesticides that an organic gardener is permitted to use to control pests and diseases. It is therefore vital not to let problems get out of control and to spray at the first sign of a problem; if you are vigilant enough, you can keep any problem to a minimum. Remember, though, that you should use spraying as a last resort in your productive organic garden because some of the pesticides will also kill some beneficial insects.

Insecticides
Pyrethrum
Pyrethrum is an insecticide made from parts of plants, in this case, the flowers of *Chrysanthemum cinerariaefolium*; it also will kill pests only if it comes into contact with them. The insecticides that contain pyrethrum do not have as long a toxic period as some other insecticides, but they will kill aphids, small caterpillars, ants, and flea beetles. Crops can be harvested a day after spraying with pyrethrum because of its rapid rate of breakdown. This insecticide is also poisonous to fish and kills a wide variety of beneficial insects, including ladybugs, but bees are surprisingly unaffected.

Left: *Chrysanthemum cinerariaefolium*, natural producers of pyrethrum.
Right: Rapeseed is becoming a more common crop around the world.

Organic Slug Pellets

These are formed of ferric phosphate and are only harmful to mollusks; therefore, they will not harm wildlife, pets, or children unless eaten in very large quantities. The pellets are blue, which is generally a warning color to wildlife, and will break down into iron and phosphates as they pass into the soil, adding goodness to your plants.

Insecticidal Soap

This insecticide is made from the potassium salts of fatty acids and kills pests on contact. It breaks down very quickly after application, so can be used up to the day of harvest. The product works by breaking down the pests' protective coating and works well on soft-bodied pests such as aphids, red spider mites, caterpillars, thrips, whitefly, and mealybugs. It does not seem to affect most beneficial predatory insects except for the introduced greenhouse predators, such as *Aphidius* and *Encarsia formosa*.

Horticultural Soap ("Soft Soap")

Although made from vegetable constituents, soft soap has very similar attributes to insecticidal soap and can also be used up to the day of harvest. It will kill aphids, scale insects, red spider mites, mealybugs, and whitefly it comes into contact with.

Diatomaceous Earth

Apart from boiling water and pyrethrum, this is the only effective way of dealing with ants. This insecticide comes in powder form and absorbs the protective coating of the ants, causing them to die.

Rapeseed Oil

Rape is becoming a common agricultural crop, and oil extracted from the seed makes an insecticide that will kill aphids, thrips, scale insects, red spider mites, and whitefly.

Fungicides

Sulfur

Sulfur is used to control powdery mildew on fruit flowers and vegetables both outside and in the greenhouse. Note, however, that certain fruits are susceptible to sulfur.

Skim Milk

This works very well against rose black spot because it coats the leaf and prevents the spores from attaching themselves to the surface. It is a preventative method, not a cure. Therefore, you should begin application as soon as you notice the first signs of the disease. It will stay active for a few weeks but should be reapplied after rain. It is important to use only skim milk because the more fat in the milk, the less effective this method will be. I like to use a mixture of equal parts milk and water.

Potassium Bicarbonate

When used as a control, not as a preventative, potassium bicarbonate works well against rose black spot as well as both powdery and downy mildew on cucurbits, roses, and fruit.

Guidelines for Spraying

It is very important, whether spraying with the more potent or with the fairly nontoxic products, always to follow the same procedure. Never use the product for any other crop than those specified on the label because some crops may be damaged by some of the products. If in doubt, contact the manufacturer or the place it was purchased.

When mixing and applying the product, it is worth being as protected as possible—without feeling like something from outer space. Gloves are crucial, as it is hands that are most likely to become contaminated and that we do not usually consider the actions of, making it very easy to rub lips, face, or other parts of the body. Wearing

gloves not only protects the hands from contamination but also prevents the user from contaminating him- or herself without thinking, as the gloves will make the hands very obvious. Another very important part of the body that needs protecting is the eyes, something I'm sure most of us would rather not be without. Goggles are the easiest protective eyewear to obtain, and they are fairly inexpensive.

It is always very difficult to imagine what damage is being done when the perpetrator is not usually visible, with fine sprays being no exception. If nothing else is worn, at least use a dust mask. Dust masks are easily purchased from home-improvement and DIY stores at a low cost, and they help prevent you from inhaling a lot of the spray. The best piece of equipment to wear to prevent all spray from being inhaled is a respirator mask, which is also available at DIY stores for reasonable costs. If I can, I also wear a waterproof jacket and trousers to protect my clothing, preventing it from getting contaminated. If not, I spray as late as possible in the day, usually last thing, so that when I then enter the house I can change immediately and put my clothing straight into the washing machine.

This is not a bad method to employ, as spraying is much better for the crops themselves if carried out early or late in the day. At each end of the day, there is little strength in the sun's rays, whereas spraying in the part of the day when the sun is at its strongest will invariably cause leaves on the crops to be scorched, potentially reducing the amount of crop harvested. Also, beneficial insects are generally at their most active during the warmer parts of the day. Spraying with chemicals that kill any insect they come into contact with is best carried out when minimal damage will be done to the insects we encourage into the garden or greenhouse.

The actual spraying equipment available varies enormously, from small handheld products to much larger motorized sprayers. Never spray with any equipment that is not in perfect working order because it may be detrimental both to you and to the crop being sprayed. For obvious reasons, never spray when it is windy because the spray will be blown onto areas where it is not required and where it may cause damage, and always try to allow at least an hour for the spray to dry before applying water. Most insecticides and fungicides deteriorate once mixed and will become ineffective if left to stand for weeks, so try to mix only what is required; any leftover spray will be wasted and can harm the environment if poured away. Keep sprays only in the containers they came in, and keep these in a locked container or at worst on a high shelf out of reach of people who may be unaware of their danger.

When spraying, the most important factor to remember is that organic pesticides work on contact. Therefore, ensuring a good covering of the affected vegetables, fruit, or herbs, by spraying to give a total coverage of the upper surface of the leaves as well as the undersides of the leaves, is the only way to eradicate the pest. But remember, there is no point spraying beyond the point of "run-off," when the spray begins dripping off the end of the leaves.

Mulching

To keep vegetable, herb, and fruit crops growing and returning as much produce as possible, you must ensure they do not have competition from other plants or suffer from lack of water. In a busy productive garden, it is often not possible to hoe as often as is required, so preventing weed growth in the first place is definitely the answer. The weeds, if left to grow, will compete for water with any productive crop, as well as taking vital nutrients out of the soil. With the global need to conserve water as much as possible, as well as the extra costs involved in applying unnecessary water to the productive areas, anything that prevents gardeners from applying extra water has to be beneficial. And this is where mulches come in.

Most mulches are applied as a 2- to 3-inch (5- to 7½-cm) thick layer to the surface of the soil. This creates an almost impenetrable barrier for most weeds. As well as preventing water loss from weeds, it also helps to prevent water loss from the soil. Quite a high proportion of water is lost in evaporation from the soil surface on hot and breezy days. The mulch acts as a blanket over the soil, keeping the ground beneath it nice and moist, while almost eliminating any water evaporation. Not only does mulch conserve water, but it also provides an excellent home for a wide variety of beneficial predatory insects that need a cool place to hide during the hot, sunny summer days. The downside of this is that it also provides a home for slugs and snails, but this should not be a problem if enough predators have been encouraged into the garden.

There is a wide range of materials that can be used as mulches on both long-term and short-term crops.

Shreddings

This option is free, with all shreddings being generated from tree and shrub prunings, as well as herbaceous stems removed from the garden. If your garden is not large enough to generate enough shreddings, why not take in prunings and so on from friends and neighbors? All that is required is a good-quality shredder that will chop up these prunings into usable pieces. It is necessary to compost them down in a heap for three to six months so that they do not remove vital nitrogen from the soil surrounding a crop.

Due to the timing of pruning and cutting back herbaceous perennials, the majority of shredding will be carried out in the winter, when it is not possible to get onto the garden.

Mulch around garlic plants in an organic garden.

All I do with ours is to shred into a heap and, in winter, cover it with a piece of plastic, just to keep off the worst of the rain—the heap stays uncovered during the drier summer months. The shredded material can be used as a pathway material or as a weed suppressant around long-term crops such as soft fruit, fruit trees, artichokes, rhubarb, and so on.

Farmyard Manure

As well as being an excellent organic matter for incorporating into the soil, well-rotted farmyard manure can be used as a thick layer around crops. It has excellent weed-suppressing and moisture-retaining qualities, but is not suitable for walking on as it can be very slippery. The same principles apply with the source of farmyard manure for mulching when used as a soil conditioner, in that the farm should be "clean" to prevent importing unwanted weeds.

Farmyard manure can be used for all crops except for roots because even with the shorter-term crops it can be dug in once the crop has been harvested. It is not a good

Straw mulch protects young grapevines from cooler temperatures.

idea to apply a mulch of farmyard manure to any root crop because they will not like the extra nutrients available and will be inclined to produce forked roots. Ensure the manure is well rotted and not fresh; fresh manure is too potent and will damage crops.

Straw

Put onto the ground as a thick layer, straw will suppress weeds very well, although on windy sites this is not a good material. It can be walked on easily to reach a crop and will rot down slowly. It can be used on long-term crops, especially strawberries, or on shorter-term vegetables. Once you've harvested the crop, remove the straw and put it onto the compost heap.

Compost

If garden compost is available only in small amounts, it is preferable to use it as a soil conditioner. If, however, you are producing sufficient compost that there is enough for both applications, then it makes an excellent mulch. It needs to be spread at a depth of 2–3 inches (5–8 cm) for it to prevent weed growth, as well as conserve moisture in the soil. During the growing season, many soil organisms will begin the process of drawing the compost into the soil, thus improving it. When using it as a mulch for long-term crops, such as fruit trees, soft fruit, and so on, dig it into the ground during spring and apply a new layer. If using it on vegetables, incorporate it into the soil once you've harvested the crop.

Kitchen, or green, compost refers specifically to composted household waste. It is not good enough for seed sowing or potting, but you can use it as a soil conditioner or mulch. Because the material has been composted, there should be no weed seeds, pests, or disease still alive in it, making it safe to put onto the garden. It can be used on the same crops as garden compost.

Grass Clippings

Most gardens have a never-ending supply of grass clippings, usually having plenty left after the compost bin has been taken care of. Because it is produced during the growing season, it is ideal for use as a mulch on short- and long-term crops. The most common way that I use grass clippings is as a sheet mulch on potatoes and brassicas, which means that I apply thin but regular layers of grass clippings around these crops to suppress weeds and, more importantly, to retain moisture.

Grass clippings are usually readily available.

Because I apply the clippings in thin layers during warm weather, they tend to rot down quickly and thus do not produce the slimy, smelly mess that appears in thick or slowly rotting layers. It is not suitable to be walked on regularly because it may be slippery. At the end of the growing season, incorporate the grass clippings into the ground as you turn the soil over during the potato harvest. With brassica crops, lightly till the clippings into the soil or leave them until you cultivate the soil.

Leaf Mold

The big problem with leaves is that there always seems to be plenty when they fall from the trees, yet there always seems to be so little once they are rotted down. At Barnsdale, we have a lot of trees, but they never generate enough leaf mold to satisfy our requirements. This material is such a valuable resource in the garden because of its structure and balanced nutrient levels that it should be used as a seed or potting soil rather than put on the garden. If there is plenty of leaf mold to go around, you can use it in the same way that you use garden compost.

Bark

Bark is a by-product of the wood industry and best used on more permanent crops because it takes a considerable time to rot down. Ultimately, you can incorporate it into the soil, usually after about three years, and replace it with a fresh layer. Applied at a depth of 2–3 inches (5–8 cm), it prevents most weeds from pushing through, keeping long-term crops weed-free as well as helping to conserve moisture. Bark provides an excellent cover for many of the beneficial insects that are essential to any organic garden.

You can likely obtain wood shavings for free from a lumber yard.

Wood Shavings

Wood shavings are another waste product from the lumber industry, and most lumber yards are only too happy for somebody to take it away. Wood shavings make excellent mulches in more sheltered gardens but can be a problem in gardens that are affected by the wind because they are so light. Wood shavings also make excellent pathway material and will rot down slowly, only having to be topped once a year. They are ideal for the longer-term crops.

Gravel

You can incorporate gravel into the soil to improve drainage and use it as a mulch to prevent weed growth as well as to conserve moisture. It does not rot down, obviously, and you'll need to top it up occasionally if you walk on it regularly. There is no problem with gravel becoming incorporated into the soil, particularly clay-based soil, because gravel can only improve the soil.

Landscape Glass

Landscape glass is suitable only for permanent areas because it does not want to be incorporated into the soil and will not rot down. If you walk on it often, you may need to top it up from time to time.

Thinning and Harvesting

Removing fruit from trees in the garden is something that a lot of gardeners do not do or even think about. It is wrong to think that a tree laden with hundreds of tiny fruits will carry all of those fruits right through until harvest. There will always be a limit as to how many fruits a tree can carry until harvest as well as the ultimate size of those fruits when picked. Most trees carrying fruit will shed some of those fruits, usually in early to midsummer, in order to lighten the load. If most tree fruits are left to ripen, the tree may still drop what it cannot carry, and very often a bit more. Thinning of tree fruits therefore ensures an even and large enough crop of well-sized fruits over the whole tree.

Thinning

Apples and pears produce fruit in clusters, and right in the center of these clusters is the "king fruit." This fruit is larger than the rest in the cluster, and removing just this is usually sufficient when it comes to thinning, with the tree producing an excellent crop of smaller fruits. If you require larger fruits, the remainder of the cluster needs to be thinned down to one or two fruits per cluster. The size of fruit that will be ultimately harvested is down to personal preference, so tailor your thinning technique to match this. It always seems such a drastic step to be removing most of the small fruits from a tree, but the weight of the resulting crop at harvest will be the same. It is just that the fewer fruits left to develop, the larger they will be when picked, and vice versa. Thinning of apples and pears can be carried out at any time from the blossom ending for a period of about four weeks.

Peaches are among the fruit crops that do not require thinning.

Cherries, peaches, and nectarines usually produce a crop that will not burden the tree, so there is no thinning required. Apricots, however, can produce an abundant crop in a good year that will require some thinning of the fruit so that the remaining fruits develop and ripen. Thinning is best left until after the natural fruit drop has occurred, about mid-spring, when the remaining fruits can be thinned so that there is about 2–4 inches (5–10 cm) between them.

Plums and damsons very often produce such an abundant crop that this can cause branches laden with fruit to snap completely from the tree. It is therefore essential to thin the fruits of these trees to prevent this, or to make sure that the branches of the tree are supported with stakes. After their natural fruit drop in midsummer, the fruits can be thinned so that they are about 3 inches (8 cm) apart. This results in good-sized juicy fruits at harvest.

Harvesting

The storage life of all fruit will depend primarily on whether or not the fruit was initially picked correctly; incorrectly harvested fruit will deteriorate very quickly. The storage of the fruit can be short term, where they are placed in a fruit bowl for eating quickly, or long term for fruits placed in storage, to be eaten over a period of months. No fruit picked from a tree can cope with being handled roughly, so a gentle approach is required.

To check whether the fruits are ready for harvest, select a fruit and lift it, usually with a cupped hand, then either continue to lift gently or lift gently while twisting slightly. If the fruit is ready, it will come away from the tree easily, but if it shows resistance to these actions, it is not fully ripe and should be left in situ. When the fruits are ready to be picked, harvesting should be carried out with a container such as a basket, bucket, or something similar that has a soft bottom to it. If the container has a hard or rough bottom, line it with a cloth or towel so that the fruits have a soft base on which to sit. Once you have removed the fruits from the tree, place them carefully in the container and, once the bottom layer has been completed, place any subsequent fruits on top of each other with extra care. If fruits are dropped onto each other, even from a low height, this will cause the fruits to bruise, shortening their storage time. When the container is full, take out the fruits with exactly the same care that was applied when putting them in in the first place. It may seem like overkill to be so precise, but it will make such an enormous difference to the time they are ideal for eating once harvested.

Chapter 5

Produce Storage and Off-Season Maintenance

Recycling

Compost is one of the best soil conditioners there is. It is by far the easiest form of organic matter to obtain for use in the garden because every productive organic garden and kitchen produce enough waste to keep at least one compost bin full right through the year. By recycling garden and kitchen waste, everything that goes into the compost bin will end up producing a soil conditioner that should be rich in nutrient content as well as being good bulky material to improve the soil.

It is the microscopic aerobic bacteria within the compost heap that will break down the material in the heap into the final friable compost. These bacteria are fueled by heat and the nitrogen found in the heap; the more nitrogen, the faster and better they work. Therefore, in order to aim for three heaps of usable compost per year, it is important to add plenty of material that is high in nitrogen. High-nitrogen materials are called "activators" and need to be added at regular intervals to the heap.

For maximum decomposition, add the material to the heap in thin layers. Fine-leaved materials such as grass clippings will compact down too much, causing anaerobic bacteria to work; more bulky items will cause the heap to cool due to the air spaces created. When it comes to composting, aerobic bacteria = good and anaerobic bacteria = bad.

You can compost flowers, leaves, and other waste from your garden.

What to Use on the Compost Heap

There are many materials that can be used in an organic compost heap. Some are fairly obvious; others are not.

Garden Waste and Old Cut Flowers

All leaves, dead flowers, and the like that you remove or that fall naturally from vegetables, fruits, and plants—even diseased and pest-infected material—can be composted. The heat generated in most compost heaps, and certainly in enclosed heaps, has been found to be high enough to kill most diseases, spores, pests, and eggs. It is important to shred this type of garden waste first because it usually contains high levels of lignin that bacteria find hard to break down and thus will be slower to rot.

Grass Clippings

Most gardeners generate a good supply of grass clippings throughout the growing season, so it is a good thing that the clippings serve as an excellent activator for the soil heap. Put thin layers onto the heap regularly; layers that are too thick will cause anaerobic bacteria to work, creating a smelly and slimy mess that rots slowly.

Raw Kitchen Vegetable Scraps

After lawn clippings, raw vegetable scraps are probably the most popular materials for the compost bin.

Rhubarb Leaves

The leaves of this plant are poisonous, so eat the stems and put the leaves onto the compost heap. Although the leaves are poisonous to us, they are perfectly safe to compost.

Garden Prunings and Hedge Clippings

It is possible to put the softer material straight on the heap, although it is generally better to shred it first. Woodier stems will compost much more slowly because they contain lignin, so you will definitely need to shred them first. Be aware of conifers and evergreens because larger quantities of them tend to make the compost more acidic.

Newspaper and Cardboard

Colored ink or colored cardboard can contain chemicals that organic gardeners do not want on their productive areas, so use only white paper with black ink or noncolored

Vegetable trimmings and eggshells are among the kitchen waste that you can compost.

cardboard. Although they are usable for compost, newspaper and cardboard do not really add anything to the heap and are probably better used for other purposes in the garden, such as being put into the bean trench or made into sweet pea tubes.

Brassica Stems

The stems of all brassicas can go onto the compost heap, but they are thick, fibrous, and full of lignin. Shredding them first is the obvious answer, but if you don't have access to a shredder, then break up the stems with a hammer—which can serve as an excellent stress buster!

Stems of brassicas, such as broccoli, should be shredded before composting.

Wood Ash

If you have a wood-burning stove, you can add all of the ash produced to the heap; however, if the ash contains material from a coal and wood fire, be warned that too much will acidify the heap. The only downside of this material is that you generate it mostly during the winter and use it primarily in the summer, so you would need to store it in bags until you are ready to put it on the heap. Wood ash will provide the heap with a good source of potassium.

Wood ash is also a fantastic barrier against ground-traveling slugs and snails. I know that a lot of people use crushed eggshells, coarse gravel, and coffee grounds, but they just make the slugs'/snails' journey uncomfortable. Wood ash actually prevents them from getting to your valuable plants because it absorbs the slime they use to travel on, effectively removing their mode of transport. It is important to use pure wood ash, no coal added, and apply it in a 4–6-inch (10–15-cm) band. You will need to reapply it after any rain (light or heavy) or heavy dew because it will become crusted and, therefore, ineffective. This is a great use for the by-product of a wood-burning stove. The added bonus is that it also has a good potash level, which helps slug/snail-susceptible plants, such as delphiniums, lupins, and dicentra, flower.

Blood Meal

Blood meal, or dried blood, is available from garden centers and home-improvement stores, generally in powder form. It contains readily available nitrogen and is an excellent activator for aerobic bacteria. It adds no bulk to the heap, but if your composting seems to be going slowly, you can sprinkle on some blood meal to give the bacteria a boost.

Natural Fabrics, Feathers, and Human and Animal Hair

All of these materials contain available nitrogen and are activators, but they are slow to break down. Therefore, before adding any of these materials to the heap, cut them into small pieces or strips so that they can be more easily broken down.

Bracken

This is a rampant plant that is commonly found in woodlands. Before collecting bracken, make sure that the woods are not privately owned and that it is OK for you to collect bracken from where you find it. It is an excellent bulking-up material for a compost heap, although it needs to be shredded first due to its high lignin content.

Hay and Straw

Hay is much better than straw as a compost material because it contains more nutrients and rots down quicker; both need to be well moistened before adding to the heap. Unless there is a very generous farmer close by, hay and straw would usually have to be bought, making them an expensive option.

Comfrey Leaves (Symphytum officinale)

I have a small patch of comfrey in my community garden area and find it invaluable. I cut the leaves regularly, which keeps the plants under control. Added to the compost heap, they work as activators and as valuable sources of potassium and phosphate. You can also put the leaves into water to create liquid feed. Every productive garden should have at least one comfrey plant.

Tree Leaves

These are not the best material to add to a compost heap that needs to be turned around quickly. Tree leaves are usually very slow to rot because they comprise mainly lignin and will take a minimum of a year, but usually two or three years, to decompose completely. If they are rotted down in plastic bags or in their own specially-built leaf bin, they make an excellent seed or potting soil.

Healthy potato stems can be put on the regular heap, while diseased stems require the heat of an enclosed bin to kill the spores.

Potato Stems

Once you've harvested the potatoes, you can put the stems onto the compost heap. If there has been blight on a particular variety, be sure to compost the haulms from these plants only on a heap in an enclosed bin because the enclosure will generate sufficient heat to kill the disease spores.

Nettles

Just as with comfrey, every gardener should have a small patch of nettles. If left to grow in a position out of sight, nettles make excellent hosts for beneficial insects as well as activators in the compost heap because they are high in nitrogen and other minerals.

Spent Hops

Apart from the beer, this is one excellent reason for living close to a brewery. Spent hops add bulk and valuable nutrients to the compost heap, and I am sure most brewers would be only too pleased if organic gardeners offered to remove the hops for them.

Cow and Horse Manure

Both fresh cow and horse manure are high in nitrogen and hence make excellent activators, and they also add bulk to the heap. They are particularly good if bulky

When Is It Ready?

When ready, the compost should almost look like soil and smell like nectar to any organic gardener. It can then be added to the vegetable plot, fruit orchard, or herb garden.

material is in short supply. Both of them also make an excellent soil conditioner quickly if left to rot in their own heap.

Pet Manure

Small animal manures from rabbits, hamsters, gerbils, guinea pigs, and the like are fine to add to the heap. While cat and dog manures do add valuable nutrients to a compost heap, they also contain other organisms that can be harmful to humans and especially children, as well as possessing the obvious disadvantage of the smell. They are best kept off the compost heap.

Urine

Urine is an excellent activator for the compost heap because it is very high in nitrogen and potassium. If you are fortunate to have young children that are potty training, you will be able to maintain a good high temperature for your compost heap.

Weeds

Compost only annual weeds that are not in flower and perennial weeds that have been lifted and left on the top of the ground to wilt and dry completely before being added to the compost heap. If annuals are coming up to flower, cut off the flower buds and add the rest of the plant. Do not add pernicious weeds to the compost heap.

Sheep Manure

Sheep manure is also an excellent activator, being high in nitrogen and most nutrients.

Poultry Manure

Poultry manure contains much higher rates of nitrogen than other manures and will make a fiery compost.

Pig Manure and Seaweed

Pig manure and seaweed can both be added to the compost heap, having the same qualities as mentioned in "Soil Preparation" on pages 42 and page 43 in Chapter 2.

What Not to Use on the Compost Heap

There are several items that should not be added to a compost heap. Some of these things are not used because they are harmful, while others simply have no beneficial effect.

Cooked Vegetables

Cooked vegetables tend to putrefy in a compost heap and will only act to attract rats.

Meat and Fish

Cooked or raw, meat and fish will have the same detrimental effect as cooked vegetables on your compost heap.

Soil

Soil does not add anything to the compost heap and is much better suited to growing crops.

Meat, raw or cooked, will be detrimental to your compost.

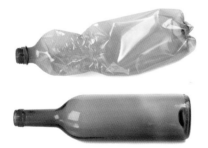

Glass, Plastic, Metal, and Stone

Obviously, none of these materials will break down and so are useless in the compost heap.

Dog and Cat Manure

As already mentioned when talking about pet manure, dog and cat manure are not suitable for a compost heap.

Weeds

The one thing we do not want to do is to spread these weeds around the garden when we use the compost, so unless they are completely desiccated first, pernicious weeds are out. The same goes for weeds in flower or seeding.

Wood Products

Wood products are slow to break down, so compost them in a separate heap and use for mulching.

How to Compost

There are several methods that you can employ to compost materials.

Compost Bin

The best type of compost bin is an enclosed one that will trap all the heat created by the rotting process within the heap and keep the bacteria working to their maximum over most of that material. An enclosed bin with a lid will produce compost the fastest.

   If a slatted side or open-sided bin is used, the contact with the air will naturally lower the temperature of the outer edge, causing the bacteria in that area to work at a slower rate. To combat this, line the inside of the compost bin with cardboard to act as an insulator as well as ultimately break down into the compost itself.

If you are composting leaves, the easiest method is to pound in four posts and wrap chicken wire around them. There is no need to spend vast sums of money on buying or building a closed bin for leaves because they are slow to compost. If need be, cardboard could be put around the sides and an old carpet or sheet of plastic put over the surface to speed up the process.

Open Heap

This is where the material is just piled into a heap and left to rot. The bacteria in the middle of such a heap will work quickly, but the ones on the outer edges will not. It is a usable method if you do not have dedicated compost bins, but it will not create three heaps in a year.

Red worms (not earthworms) are effective composters.

Sheet Composting

People without an area to compost can employ this method because it involves spreading thin layers of compostable material between vegetable rows and leaving it to rot in situ. This also saves on the hard work involved with composting in the first two ways. This method works well with longer-term crops.

Worm Composting

Worm composting, or vermicomposting, works well in both store-bought bins and homemade ones, and you could even use old trash cans successfully. Place a small amount of composting material in the bottom of the bin and add red wiggler worms (not earthworms) at this stage. As before, add the material in thin layers at regular intervals—the worms convert this into usable compost. In specially made bins, the usable compost falls out when ready and can be used immediately. Bins without this facility will need to be emptied once the worms have worked their way to the top.

✦ ✦ ✦ ✦

If using any of the first three methods to compost waste materials, you can speed up the process by regularly turning the bin (emptying it and then filling it back up with the same materials) or moving the heap from one place to another—your goal is to mix up the materials, which ensures that all of the material is composted and at the fastest possible rate. You need to do this once every month during spring, summer, and autumn, and probably once every six weeks during the winter.

With all of the composting methods, it is important for the bacteria to work at their best to maximize the heat in the heap. Just as important is keeping the heap moist. Closed or covered heaps will need water applied to them from time to time. The bacteria also work better in an alkaline heap, and periodic applications of lime will help to keep the pH at a favorable level; however, adding a good mixture of materials to the heap should give the right environment. Still, if you add coniferous or evergreen waste to the heap, it may be wise to counterbalance their acidic properties with a handful of lime.

Storing Your Produce

The storage of any produce is crucial, as it will extend the time for which we are able to draw on the maximum amount of available vegetables, fruit, and herbs. The primary aim is to ensure that these stored vegetables will be on hand during the winter months when the availability of fresh produce is not at its greatest, thereby providing a greater choice for meal times. When mentioning the storage of any produce, it is done so without taking into consideration the use of a freezer. Most fruit, vegetables, and herbs will store better using traditional methods than in the more modern chest freezer.

The most important point to note about storing vegetables, fruit, and herbs is to store only perfectly healthy produce. Each item should be carefully checked before being stored. Any produce with blemishes or mechanical damage, or showing signs of rotting, needs to be eaten immediately or disgarded rather than stored, as it will potentially rot and affect perfectly healthy crops in the process.

The storage conditions for most fruit and vegetables are fairly similar in that they generally require a cool, dark place to keep for the maximum time. The coolness of storage will slow the maturing or ripening process of the produce. For longer storage, the cooler, the better, as long as it remains frost-free. If the produce does become frosted, it will generally turn into an inedible mush. Darkness also helps to reduce the maturing and ripening process. Usually, a garage or shed is ideal for storing fruit and vegetables, as long as it is free from rodents. Most produce will be stored in containers, although for large amounts of potatoes or root crops, a straw clamp can be used. If straw is readily

Select only healthy, unblemished produce for storage.

available, pile the crop into a heap and pack the straw over it as insulation from frost. Due to the looseness and lightness of straw, it is best kept in bales or held in place by a tarpaulin cover. Move the straw and remove any produce as and when it is required.

Onions, Shallots, and Garlic

It is important when growing onions, shallots, and garlic for storage to select the varieties grown carefully. Some varieties do not store well, while others will store for several months. Taste is all-important to me, but so is the supply of these bulbs throughout the winter and early spring. I therefore grow varieties that I like, but that do not store well, which will be harvested and eaten first. While the taste of varieties that store well is important, it is secondary to their ability to store. In this way I have a good early crop of onions to eat, as well as bulbs that last until February or March in storage. The length a storing variety will last in storage is determined by the variety itself (some store longer than others) in combination with them being correctly grown, harvested, and dried prior to storing.

The most important first step is to ensure that the stems of each bulb are allowed to fall over of their own free will. Do not be tempted to bend over the stems before they are ready, under the false pretense that this will enable the crop to be lifted early, dried in the sunnier weather and stored. Trying to rush the process artificially only results in the storage life of the bulbs being shortened.

Once the stems of the onions, shallots, and garlic have fallen over, gone brown, and withered on the whole row, they are ready to be lifted. To harden the skin and extend store time, the bulbs then need to be dried. I find that the easiest way is first, as the tops of the bulbs start to bend, to carefully pull some of the soil away from the bulb to expose as much of it as possible to the sun, to start the drying process. When they are ready to be lifted, I build a very simple drying bed consisting of four posts and a piece of chicken wire. I pound in the four posts and attach the chicken wire to it with "U" nails so that it is tight, but not completely inflexible. The wire cradle really needs to be 18–24 inches (45–60 cm) from the ground to allow good air circulation.

If the weather turns very wet and it looks as if this is likely to last for several days, the onions, shallots, and garlic need to be brought inside to complete the drying process under cover. I usually use a polyethylene tunnel for this, but a lean-to, shed, or similar structure will do the same job. After a couple of weeks, the bulbs will have dried enough to store. The easiest and cheapest way is to ask for some netted onion bags from a fruit and vegetable vendor at a farmers' market and store the bulbs in these. Before storing in netted bags, remove and discard the brown withered bulb tops. They can then be stored in a cool, dark place on slatted benches or, better still, hanging up where they will get excellent air circulation. The second way of storing is to tie them up into long strands or bunches, as seen in the supermarkets with garlic.

Potatoes

This is an easy crop to store and will potentially last until February or March. As with their growing conditions, stored potatoes will turn green if exposed to light, so they need

to be stored in a dark place. It is also important to use paper bags that are not coated with any waxy substances; the bag must be able to breathe so that the potatoes inside do not sweat and ultimately rot. Burlap bags are very good, but only if the potatoes are stored in complete darkness. This is because the bags are woven and will therefore allow light through.

Once lifted, the main-crop potatoes for storage must be left on the soil surface to dry for a day or so. It is important to remove as much of the soil from each potato as possible while harvesting. This soil not only adds weight to the bag but also potentially harbors pests—as well as being very messy when you ultimately clean the potatoes prior to cooking. The drying on the soil surface hardens the skin and extends the storage time.

Just as with onions, shallots, and garlic, there are some varieties of potato that store better than others, so research prior to ordering is vital. Once the potatoes have dried, sort them into perfect tubers for storage and imperfect ones to be eaten first. Due to their different uses, I always store only one variety of potato to a bag. After filling, the bag is tied at the top, the potato variety written on the side of a bag, and the bag taken into storage. To prevent any rotting from a damp floor, I like to stand my bags on an old wooden pallet, which allows good air circulation around the whole bag. The bags can then be opened and potatoes taken as required, always remembering to reseal the bag to prevent the potatoes from turning green.

Parsnips

It has long been a belief held by gardeners that the sweetness in parsnips is obtained by the roots being subjected to a good, hard, and penetrating frost. This may or may not be the case, but the fact is that if the ground is frozen solid and parsnips are on the menu, there is no chance whatsoever of getting them out of the ground to eat. This is

where short- and long-term storage becomes essential. Short-term storage involves digging up a few parsnips every week and storing them in a loosely filled trench, as with leeks, so that they can be easily harvested from there when required, even after a particularly hard frost. The method of long-term storage is identical to that for all the other root crops.

Root Crops

Most of the root crops, such as carrot, beet (beetroot), celeriac, rutabaga (swede), kohlrabi, turnip, scorzonera, and salsify can be stored for a lengthy period by using this method. Each of the crops, once harvested, needs to be cleaned of as much soil as possible without damaging the roots. This removes any harboring pests, as well as enabling the roots to be checked for damage. With all of the root types, with the exception of beets (beetroot), the tops should be cut off with a sharp knife as close to the top of the root as possible. If too much top growth is left on, this may potentially rot, possibly causing the rest of the root to rot from the top downward. Beets (beetroot), however, will "bleed" if the leaf stems are cut cleanly, limiting their storage potential. Therefore, it is best to hold the root firmly while twisting the tops until they tear, leaving approximately 1 inch (2½ cm) of top on the root. The leaf stems of beets (beetroot) do not seem to rot in storage.

Once the roots have been cleaned and the tops dealt with, the roots are ready for storing. The container used to store them in can be a deep tray, wooden box, or large planter—in fact, anything that can be moved, if required, and will contain the packing material. Moist coarse sand, vermiculite, bark, or moist soil can be used as packing material around the roots. It is important that the packing material is kept moist (but not

wet) because this prevents the stored roots from drying out and becoming inedible, as well as helping to keep them cool. If the tray or box to be used is slatted or has regular holes that the packing material will fall through, line it with cardboard or newspaper.

Next, put a thin layer of packing material into the bottom of the tray, and lay out the first layer of roots. They need to be packed in as tightly as possible, but not touching. Another layer of material is then put over the top of these roots, ensuring that it falls between the roots and totally covers them, before repeating the laying-out process. This continues until the tray or box is full and the last layer is completely covered with the packing material. If it is a large tray or box, the filling needs to be done in situ because the container will probably be too heavy to move once filled with sand, soil, or bark.

For smaller amounts of roots, a large pot can be used. Cut a circle of cardboard to cover the drainage holes at the bottom of the pot, and cover this with a 4-inch (10-cm) layer of packing material. The roots can then be pushed into this so that they are standing vertically. Push in as many as the pot will accommodate, ensuring that they do not touch each other, and fill in around and over the tops of the roots with the packing material. When storing the roots of celeriac, I generally use a very large pot, up to 4 feet (120 cm) in diameter, because the roots tend to be quite big. I then pack in and around them with moist bark.

Once you've stored each of the roots in its appropriate container, the most important job is to label the containers; otherwise, attempting to collect produce from storage becomes a bit of hit or miss. After labeling, store in a cool, dark place—the cooler, the better, as this will slow down the regrowth of the root tops. Also, if there is a possibility of cats gaining access to the storage area, ensure that each pot is covered with a piece of cardboard held down with a stone or brick. If you do not do this, there may be an unpleasant surprise waiting for the first person to harvest produce!

Summer Squash (Marrows), Pumpkins, and Other Squash

The most important aspect when considering the storage life of pumpkins or squash is the toughness of the outer skin. In order to get the maximum storage time, the skin needs to be ripened and toughened in the late summer sun for several weeks. To get the best overall ripeness, stand each fruit on a brick, pot, or something similar that lifts it from the moist ground.

Once the skin feels tough and before the first frost, cut the fruits so that 4–6 inches (10–15 cm) of stalk is left on the fruit. The stalk dries and hardens very quickly, protecting the neck of the fruit in storage. The fruits are then stored in a cool, dry place in a position where they receive excellent air circulation; sitting on slatted shelves or an old wooden pallet would be ideal. If ripened for long enough, summer squash (marrows) can last two to three months in storage, while pumpkins and winter squashes can be stored for up to nine months.

Hot Peppers

Hopefully, by the end of the summer, a greenhouse-raised crop will be laden with an abundance of hot peppers. Harvest and either dry on the onion cradle, if the weather permits, or on the greenhouse benching for at least a couple of weeks. Once dried, store in sealed airtight jars, where they will last for several years.

Celery

Self-blanching celery cannot be stored outside because it is produced above ground and will therefore succumb to frost. It can be lifted and plunged into vermiculite, soil, or bark, where it will last for two to three weeks. Blanched or trench celery, however,

is buried in the ground and the tops mounded with soil, giving the plants excellent insulation against frost. These can therefore be stored in situ and dug up as and when required.

Apples and Pears

The storing procedure really starts with the correct harvesting of the fruit. Apples and pears bruise very easily, and bruised fruit will rot very quickly in storage. You therefore need to place the fruits into the harvesting basket, bucket, or bag very carefully when harvesting. Under no circumstances should fruits be dropped onto one another. Bruising of the fruit will start to show only after the fruits have been stored.

As with all stored produce, it important to check the crop and select only the perfect fruits for storage. Place these fruits carefully into a clear plastic bag, tie up the top, and label it. To allow the fruits to breathe and lengthen their storage time, pierce the bag with a few small holes using a needle. Store in a cool, dark place. I like to place my bags on slatted shelving to allow good air circulation.

An alternative method is to individually wrap each fruit in newspaper or tissue, and place into a tray as a single layer. These are stored in the same way, ensuring with both methods that the storage spot is free from rodents.

It is important to check the fruits regularly for signs of rot or disease, and remove any showing signs of these. Apple and pear rots quickly take hold and will rapidly render perfectly healthy fruits unusable.

Herbs

Although always at their best when picked fresh, most herbs can be utilized in winter by using leaves, stems, and seeds that have been stored. The most common way of storing herbs is to dry them. This is suitable for many types, such as basil, bay, dill, mint, oregano, parsley, rosemary, sage, and thyme. Bunches are tied and hung in a dry and airy place where they can be left to dry slowly. It is important to allow them to dry naturally to maximize flavor.

Another method, and one that is gaining in popularity, primarily for the professional look it gives to a kitchen, is to infuse herbs in olive oil or vinegar. These jars or bottles are then left on display in the kitchen, and the herbs are removed as they are required. It is a method suitable for herbs such as basil or mint. Most herbs will stand in a jar of water and be happy for a few days before losing turgidity and wilting. Parsley will stand for several days in water as an alternative to using it dried. A refrigerator will also keep most herbs fresh for a few days, if they are sealed in plastic bags.

It is not only leaves and stems that can be stored. Some herbs have seeds that can be stored for either cooking or sowing the following season. For both purposes, the seed is ready to save once the seed pods have generally turned brown and begun to open. This is the sign that the seeds are ripe and can be harvested. Carefully knock them out into a paper bag and, if they are moist from rain or a heavy dew, dry them first on a piece of newspaper before storing. To preserve the seed for culinary uses, pour into an airtight jar for use whenever required. For seed to be sown the following season, either seal in the bag they were collected in or pour them into a small envelope. Remember to write the variety name on the bag or envelope, and store in a cool, dry place for use the following year.

If not totally banishing the freezer from being used for all stored produce, it is possible to freeze some herbs, such as coriander and mint, without them losing much flavor. Other herbs, such as chives, require a slightly more specialized treatment than putting in a plastic bag and placing in the freezer. Whole chive leaves do not store very well on their own, but they do store very well when cut up into small pieces and frozen in ice-cube trays. The cubes can then be added to your cooking when required, or the cubes melted and the chives used fresh in cold dishes.

Maintaining a Greenhouse

In the productive garden, one of our aims is to produce early crops because it is these that cost us the most to buy. A greenhouse is essential in achieving this. Not having a greenhouse will not prevent any gardener from getting early crops; those crops will just not be as early as those of gardeners that do have one. That said, a greenhouse is a great asset only if looked after properly, and the best time to maintain it is during early autumn when there is little going on in there.

There are several different shapes and sizes available, with some being relatively cheap and others costing considerably more. It is more often than not the case that buying cheaply can be false savings, because you really do get what you pay for. The two most important factors to consider before purchasing a greenhouse are the size

A greenhouse is essential to getting early crops.

required and whether it has adequate ventilation. It may seem a pointless statement to make with regard to the size, but all too often gardeners rush into buying a greenhouse without proper thought as to what it will be used for. Consider not only the propagation requirement but also the crops that will be grown in it once most of the indoor propagation has been carried out and, finally, how it will be used in winter. Will tender container plants be put into your greenhouse to protect them from the worst of the winter or will it stand predominantly empty from November to January?

The most important factor once the size has been determined is how the air is to be circulated around the inside. The effects of the vast majority of greenhouse diseases are worsened by lack of air movement, and they can actually be prevented with the right ventilation. The larger a structure your greenhouse is, the more roof vents and possibly side vents will be required. Is it possible to leave the doors open to aid air circulation? Most only have doors at one end, so it may be of benefit to have a motorized vent or fan at the opposite end in larger ones, to draw air through on less windy days. Our 8 x 20-foot (2⅖ x 6-m) greenhouse has a small motorized fan at the end opposite to the doors that works on a thermostat. When the temperature reaches 70°F (21°C), the fan

starts and helps to prevent the temperature from rising too much by keeping the air moving. We also have automatic vents on one that is used for houseplants that are set at the same temperature, while all the other greenhouses have manual vents. I like to have the option, where vegetables are concerned, of being able to manipulate the temperature and humidity to match the crops growing inside. It is important to oil or grease the mechanism that works the vents during the winter months when it is less full, rather than trying to do the job on a hot spring day when it is full of young plants.

If your greenhouse is connected to an electrical supply, it must be fitted with waterproof outdoor electrical fittings; otherwise, the combination of moisture and water in general could prove fatal. If your greenhouse is heated using these electrical points, it is advisable to have an electrician check all heaters and other electrical equipment annually. This check should be carried out in late summer or early autumn, prior to any heaters being used, to keep the greenhouse frost-free, as time must be left for any work required. I like thermostatically controlled heaters that either blow cold air, with the heat only coming on once the temperature drops below the point at which it has been set, or a heater that is turned on but blows hot air only once the temperature has dropped below that all-important setting. Both of these heaters are cheap to run on the cold setting, so can be used to help circulate air in the summer.

Depending on the power rating of the heater, it will manage to heat only a certain-sized greenhouse, so be sure to check the heating capabilities before buying. It is also possible to heat your greenhouse with a kerosene or gas heater, with the latter requiring some ventilation to prevent a buildup of gases harmful to the plants. Both of these types of heater require regular checks on their fuel to prevent them from going out in the middle of a very cold night, resulting in all the plants in the greenhouse being lost.

During early autumn, check all the glass to ensure none has slipped and that none of the panes has cracked or broken. Apart from being dangerous, all of these things can cause problems during winter by allowing cold air in, potentially damaging any early crops. Once all the glass has been checked and any slipped or damaged panes rectified, wash the glass. If any white shading has been painted onto the glass earlier in the year, to protect the crops inside from the strong summer sunlight, remove it at this time to ensure maximum penetration through the glass of the much less powerful winter sun. Glass also gets a covering film of dirt or algae during the year that needs to be removed for the same reason. There are two ways of cleaning the outside: either with a

Some crops, such as peas, can be started in the greenhouse as early as November.

brush; hot, soapy water; and plenty of elbow grease or with a pressure washer. It is not only important to remove light-blocking dirt from the glass, but also to get rid of any pest eggs or disease spores lodged in the cracks and crevices in the framework.

Usually by the end of September, most of the crops have been removed from the greenhouse and anything left can be moved out for a day without any lasting damage occurring. This is the ideal time to clean the inside, using either of the methods used for cleaning the exterior. I like to use a combination of the two methods by washing the glass and framework down with a soft brush, bucket of hot water, and environmentally friendly bleach. This takes off most of the dirt as well as killing many disease spores, while the power washing that follows will remove the remaining pest eggs or disease spores, as well as any stubborn dirt. The excess water lying on the floor can be brushed out to leave the roof, sides, and floor spotless.

As soon as the inside has been cleaned, it is worth insulating the greenhouse for winter, whether it is heated or not. It is quite simple to do, with the easiest and cheapest material being plastic bubble wrap. Most greenhouses are made to accommodate insulation, and you can buy special clips for attaching the plastic bubble wrap to the vertical bars of the framework from most garden centers. It is the air trapped in the bubbles that helps to keep the cold out and the heat in, making a significant reduction in heating bills as well as maintaining a higher nighttime temperature in an unheated greenhouse. Once a heater is no longer required, and certainly by the end of May, the insulation can be removed, cleaned, and stored for use during the forthcoming winter.

Staging is an excellent accessory, as it means work can be carried out at a reasonable height, reducing the need to bend. Any bench needs to be strong enough to cope with its planned use, and the top of the bench needs to be about 36 inches (90 cm) high for most gardeners, to make working on it less stressful on back muscles. If required, heat can be installed on this bench to speed up germination of vegetable and herb seeds. There are two methods that can be employed, either installing heated cable into sand or laying out a heat mat, both of which have their temperatures controlled by a thermostat.

If you are using the heated-cable method, the staging must be strong enough to cope with the weight of sand used. Put a layer of coarse sand onto the base of the staging, and lay out the heated cable in loops across the surface. Cover the cable with a layer of coarse sand and level off the top. Once a year, it is worth just scraping off the very surface layer of sand and replacing it with fresh to eliminate a buildup of algae and weeds. Any weeds found growing in the sand will need to be removed as soon as they are spotted and certainly before they get a chance to seed themselves around.

When installing a heat mat onto staging, put a 2-inch (5-cm) sheet of styrofoam onto the bench first; this acts as an insulator, ensuring that all the valuable heat is directed upward. Next, place the heat mat on top of the styrofoam and cover with thick plastic, which will protect the mat from water as well as mechanical damage. Seed trays and pots can then be placed directly onto the plastic, but I like to use a layer of capillary matting between the trays and the plastic. As there is a good heat coming up from below the trays, the soil in those trays will dry from the bottom upward, but using capillary matting greatly reduces this problem when the matting is kept moist. Each year, carefully clean the heated matting and plastic using environmentally friendly bleach and hot water; the capillary matting will last only one season before it has to be replaced.

Regular Maintenance

Maintenance of a greenhouse is not just confined to early autumn. There are plenty of jobs to carry out during the main growing season, from January to October. As soon as propagation starts, the greenhouse requires regular attention to get the best from these crops. Although I like to start some of the peas and fava (broad) beans in November,

Open windows to ventilate your greenhouse as temperatures require.

the real work does not start until January, with the heated bench being almost full by the end of the month. Regular jobs will include the following:

- If the greenhouse is heated, always check the heater every time it is used.
- Check seed packets for optimum germination temperature of seeds before placing onto a heat mat or into a propagator.
- If using capillary matting, keep it moist by wetting twice a day.
- Be vigilant and remove any pest or disease as soon as it is visible.
- Damp down on hot days by pouring water onto the floor at least twice a day. This increases the humidity around the leaves of the plants inside and prevents excessive water loss. It also helps prevent the spread of red spider mite.
- Either paint special greenhouse shading on the outside of the glass or erect netted shading over your crop as the strength of the sun increases, usually during June.
- Check the supports on fruiting vegetables, such as tomatoes, cucumbers, and melons, as the fruits increase in size to ensure they are still capable of carrying the crop.
- Ventilate on hotter days.

Chapter 6

DIY Projects for Your Garden

Virtually all of the items that follow can be bought off the shelf from most good garden centers, DIY stores, and certainly from an abundance of companies selling via the Internet. I find, however, that making my own is not only extremely satisfying but also an awful lot cheaper, which leaves me more money to spend on the essentials I cannot make. It is worth remembering that most horticultural sundries have been made to standard specifications and will not necessarily be ideal for all gardeners, whereas homemade equivalents can be adapted to fit exactly the position, system, or task for which they are required.

Grow Tunnel

A grow tunnel, sometimes called a low tunnel or tunnel cloche, is a very adaptable piece of equipment because it can be made to varying widths and lengths. It basically consists of a number of hoops and polyethylene (plastic), which means that the length is variable and any excess plastic not required for that particular crop is not cut, but can be folded up. In this way, when more hoops and a longer tunnel are required, the plastic sheet is still usable. Although the hoops for this type of tunnel can be made by bending strong galvanized wire into the curved shapes required, I prefer to use polyethylene pipe, which is much easier to use and much stronger. This water pipe is easily available from home improvement and hardware stores.

Due to the systems we employ at Barnsdale, a grow tunnel that covers a width of 4 feet (120 cm) is ideal. Not only does it accommodate the bed system we employ in certain parts of the productive gardens, but also it works well for a lot of the crops grown in rows. Mind you, we have also cut shorter lengths of pipe to cover the individual rows of smaller crops, where a larger tunnel would be overkill, so that we can be as adaptable as possible. A grow tunnel covering the 4-foot (120-cm) width is used as an example here; you can make yours to the width required by adjusting the length the pipe is cut. I have found that the 1-inch (25-mm) water pipe is strong enough for most grow tunnels, although, if you are gardening on a very windy site, 1¼ inches (32 mm) may be better. When you no longer need the grow tunnel for a certain crop, you can easily dismantle it and move it to another crop.

Dimensions	Materials	Tools
Height: 2 feet (60 cm)	Polyethylene (MDPE) water pipe	Saw
Width: Variable	Bamboo canes	Pruning shears
Depth: Variable	2-inch (5-cm) nails	Drill
	Strong string	Scissors or knife
	Plastic sheeting	

Instructions

1. Cut the pipe into 6½-foot (2-m) lengths and cut as many pipes as will be needed, bearing in mind that they will be spaced 24 inches (60 cm) apart. Into each end of these lengths of polyethylene pipe, insert a 9-inch (23-cm) piece of bamboo cane, so that approximately half is sticking out of the pipe. This piece of cane makes pushing the hoops into the ground much easier, as well as helping to anchor them. The canes can be cut easily with a pair of pruning shears.

2. Drill a hole across each end of the pipe, about 2 inches (5 cm) from the end, at right angles to the direction the hoop will go over the crop, and large enough to hold a 2-inch (5-cm) screw or nail very firmly. The hoops are now ready to be pushed into the ground at a spacing of approximately 24 inches (60 cm) apart, ensuring that the screws/nails are just above soil level.

3. Set out all the hoops to their longest run, so that the plastic sheeting can be cut at its maximum length for use throughout the whole season on the varying crops being grown. To ensure the hoops do not move, tie a piece of strong string to a 12-inch (30-cm) piece of bamboo cane, which is pushed into the ground at an angle, just under one of the end hoops. Loop the string once around the apex of each hoop in turn.

4. Keep the string tight at all times, right along the total run, then tie the end to another piece of bamboo cane, which can be pushed into the ground, at an angle, under the opposite end hoop. Another method is to drill a hole right through the apex of the hoop and use bamboo canes pushed through the holes so that they run the complete length of the tunnel, forming a solid top ridge. Place the plastic over the hoops, gather each end, and bury each in the ground, ensuring that the plastic is as tight as possible right along the run of hoops.

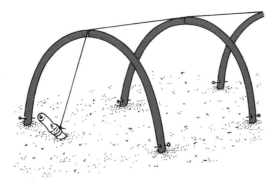 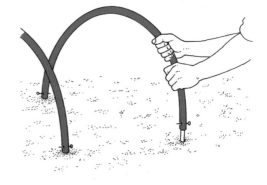

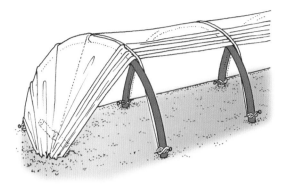

5. The last job is to tie a piece of string onto the nail or screw inserted into the end of the hoops, pull the string across the plastic to the other nail or screw on the opposite side of the hoop, and tie it onto that. Carry out this procedure with all the hoops. Make sure that the end hoops each have string across the side of the hoop that faces into the center of the grow tunnel. This string not only keeps the plastic from flapping around in the wind and potentially tearing, but also holds it in place when raised on each side of the hoops to allow ventilation.

Deep Bed Cloche

The grow tunnel is ideal when you require adaptability, but if the beds to be used are symmetrical or of a standard shape, a more rigid cloche can be made. In our parterre garden at Barnsdale, there are triangular, rectangular, and square beds laid out in a symmetrical fashion. Each of the same-shaped beds are also exactly the same size, raised 4 inches (10 cm) from the ground, using 4 x 1 inch (10 x 2 ½ cm) rough-sawn lumber, and are of a number that divides well into a four-year crop rotation plan. As the size of each shape does not vary, it is possible to build rigid cloches that will fit exactly over the rectangular and square beds when required. I find that a cloche made to fit a 4-foot (120-cm) square bed is manageable by one person, but anything larger will require two people to lift the cloche on and off.

Dimensions	Materials	Tools
Height: 2 feet (60 cm) Width: 4 feet (120 cm) Depth: 4 feet (120 cm)	2 x 2-inch (5 x 5-cm) rough-sawn lumber 4-inch (10-cm) screws Bamboo canes 1-inch (25-mm) polyethylene (MDPE) water pipe Batten Plastic sheeting 2-inch (5-cm) nails	Saw Screwdriver Drill Pruning shears Scissors or knife Hammer

Instructions

1. Use 2 x 2-inch (5 x 5-cm) wood to make the base framework. Cut four pieces so that they fit as snugly as possible around the outside of the raised bed. The dimensions of the finished frame are driven by the size of the raised bed. A super-snug fit is required because often the pathways between are made from a solid material, so there will be no means of anchoring the cloche. In windy weather, this snug fit will hold the cloches in place over the raised bed.

2. Using two 4-inch (10-cm) screws at each corner, screw all four pieces of wood together, ensuring the corners are all square. Drill a hole three-quarters of the way

through the wood at each corner, and insert a 6-inch (15-cm) length of bamboo cane, leaving approximately 4 inches (10 cm) sticking upward each corner. If making a rectangular cloche, you will also need to drill the same type of holes at approximately 24 inches (60 cm) apart on each side down the length of the cloche. Use two 4-inch (10-cm) screws at each corner of the base framework to hold the framework together and all four corners square.

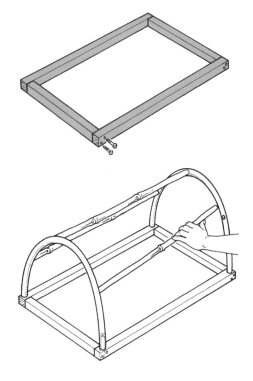

3. Cut the polyethylene pipe into the required number of hoops to a length of 6½ feet (2 m). Push one end over a cane and the other end over the cane directly opposite. This gives a nicely curved hoop that is approximately 24 inches (60 cm) above the wooden base, allowing plenty of growing height for the crops it will cover. Drill a hole at the apex large enough to accommodate a bamboo cane on the inside of the end hoops, taking care not to drill right through the other side of the hoop. Do the same on each side of these end hoops, at the point halfway between the apex and the wooden frame. (If constructing a rectangular cloche, a hole needs to be drilled right through all the other hoops at the same points as for the end ones.)

4. Into each of these holes, insert a bamboo cane cut to fit exactly between the hoops. The back of the end hoops, which have not been drilled, will hold these canes nicely in place. It is important to drill right through the middle hoops because a cane has to be passed through the hole. Make sure that if more than one cane is used for each run that they join at a point inside the hoops. If using canes seems awkward, the string method used for the grow tunnel can also be used here, with strong string stapled to the wooden base frame at one end and looped tightly around each hoop before being stapled at the opposite end.

5. Put on a piece of plastic sheeting so that it fits tightly over the hoops, and attach it to the base frame with batten. The batten needs only to be 1 x ½ inch (25 x 12 mm) in size. If the plastic is rolled around it a couple of times before nailing on, it will be more than secure. To prolong the life of the wooden base and the batten, paint with a wood preservative that has the organic seal of approval.

Planting Board

This has to be one of the simplest but most useful homemade tools any vegetable grower could hope to possess. It is important to make the measuring as straightforward as possible or else your planting board could become a frustrating tool. Combinations of the 3-inch (8-cm) saw cuts will cover most crop sowing planting distances, but if these seem too many and too confusing, just make a cut every 6 inches (15 cm) and approximate between the cuts.

The uses of this board are many. It can be used for measuring sowing or planting distances and row spacing. It can also be used for making seed furrows by using the corner of one of the long edges, as well as making an excellent supporting stick when having to bend over.

Dimensions	Materials	Tools
Length: 4 feet (120 cm) Width: 4 inches (10 cm) Depth: 1 inch (2½ cm)	Piece of smoothed wood, 3 x 1 inches (8 x 2½ cm) Galvanized roof nails	Saw Hammer

Instructions

1. Cut a piece of 3 x 1-inch (8 x 2½-cm) planed wood to a length of 4 feet (120 cm). Make a shallow crosswise saw cut 3 inches (8 cm) from the top of the length. Continue along the length of the wood at 3-inch (8-cm) spacings. This should give a piece of wood with fifteen saw cuts along its complete length.
2. Nail a single galvanized roofing nail just behind the first 12-inch (30-cm) saw cut. Just behind the 24-inch (60-cm) saw cut, hammer in two galvanized roofing nails, with three going just behind the 36-inch (90-cm) saw cut.

Note:

It is important to use nails with large, flat heads so that they can be easily seen. It will be quick and easy to calculate distances by using these nails as markers.

Firming Board

Firming boards are very useful tools when potting or sowing, and they are simple to make. With most structures and homemade equipment in the productive garden being made from wood, it is usually possible to find an extra piece of wood that measures approximately 8 x 6 inches (20 x 15 cm). This is the size of a standard half seed tray, which will make it more adaptable as it can then be used on both half and full-sized seed trays.

Dimensions	Materials	Tools
Length: 8 inches (20 cm)	Piece of lumber 8 x 6 inches (20 x 15 cm)	Wood file
Width: 6 inches (15 cm)	Wooden batten 1 x 1 inch (2½ x 2½ cm)	Saw
Depth: usually 1 inch (2½ cm)		Drill
		Screwdriver

Instructions

1. Take an extra piece of wood that measures about 8 x 6 inches (20 x 15 cm). This will be your firming board. It is important to match the inside dimensions of the seed tray, so the tips of the corners of the board will need to be cut off and rounded with a file to ensure a nice snug fit into the top part of the seed tray.
2. Cut a 1 x 1-inch (2½ x 2½-cm) piece of wood for the handle that runs the length of the board. Drill three holes into both the board and the handle and screw it into place using 1¾-inch (4-cm) screws, from the board up into the handle. The board can now be used for leveling seed and soil across the tops of seed trays, as well as firming it so that you can sow seeds.

Instructions for Round Pots

If making a firming board for round pots, cut the wood into a circle that drops into the top 1 inch (2½ cm) of the pot size to be used. There is no need to go too deep, as the board will be used only to firm soil at the very top of the pot. Attach a handle, fixing it with a screw coming from the board up into the handle.

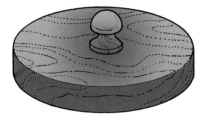

Potting Bench

A movable potting bench is a priceless piece of equipment and is very easy to make, even by a newbie do-it-yourselfer. All that is required is a piece of wood (preferably planed), some 2-inch (5-cm) screws, a wood saw, drill, screwdriver, and organic varnish.

Dimensions	Materials	Tools
Height: 12 inches (30 cm) Width: 36 inches (90 cm) Depth: 18 inches (45 cm)	Piece of wood, preferably plywood, 45 inches long x 36 inches wide x 1 inch thick (110 x 90 x 2½ cm) Eighteen 2-inch (5-cm) screws Organic varnish	Wood saw Drill Screwdriver Paintbrush

Instructions

1. Cut out four pieces of wood. The first should measure 36 x 18 inches (90 x 45 cm), the next 36 x 12 inches (90 x 30 cm) and, finally, two that are both 18 x 11 inches (45 x 27½ cm) in size. The first piece of wood is the largest and will form the base of the potting bench, with the other 36-inch (90-cm)-long piece forming the back. The final two pieces make up the sides of the bench.

2. Cut off the front top corner on each of the two sides because this is not required. If using a

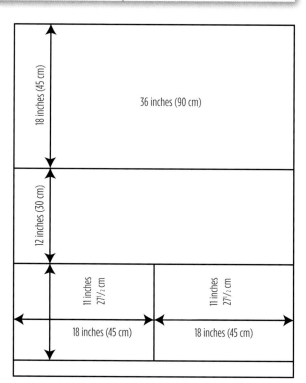

wood saw to cut the corners, leave 8 inches (20 cm) at the top back and 4 inches (10 cm) at the bottom front. If a jigsaw is available, these two side pieces can be cut with a very professional-looking curve. Drill four equidistant holes ½ inch (1 cm) in from each side of the base and screw the sides down to the base.

3. Use six screws to attach the back to the base; attach the back to the sides by drilling and then screwing through the overlapping sides and into the back of the potting bench.

4. The final job is to treat the whole potting bench because it will be subjected to plenty of moisture from the soil used. I like to use a tough varnish, as this will protect the wood not only from moisture but also from scratching and mechanical damage inflicted by pots and trays. You may need to reapply the varnish at the end of each season, depending on how much work the bench has endured. The potting bench can now be taken anywhere in the productive garden and put onto any flat surface for potting to be carried out.

Notes:

- Mark out the dimensions on the sheet of wood before starting any sawing, to limit wastage. The old adage is "measure twice, cut once".
- Use four screws to attach the sides to the base. The back will need six screws to attach it to the base and can also be attached to the sides by drilling and then screwing through the overlapping sides and into the back.

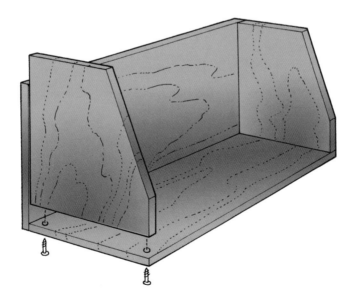

Cold Frame

Cold frames are relatively easy to make, and this is a far cheaper option than buying a similar-quality product. All that is required to make one is rough-sawn lumber in the following sizes and a few tools.

Dimensions	Materials	Tools
Size varies according to your requirement but usually no more than 4 feet (120 cm) wide	54 inches (135 cm) of 2 x 2-inch (5 x 5-cm) rough-sawn lumber 44 feet (13¹⁄₅ m) of 4 x 1¾-inch (10 x 4-cm) rough-sawn lumber in multiples of 4 feet (120 cm)—floorboards would make a good substitute 13¼ feet (4 m) of 1¾ x 1-inch (4 x 2¾ cm) rough-sawn lumber Eight 3-inch (8-cm) metal angle brackets Three 2-inch (5-cm) hinges Metal latch Sixty 2¾-inch (6-cm) wood screws Thirty-two ¾-inch (2-cm) wood screws 13¾-foot (360 cm) wooden batten Plastic sheeting 2-inch (5-cm) nails Organic wood preservative	Drill Screwdriver Wood saw Hammer Paintbrush

Instructions

1. The first job is to cut virtually all the wood into the following lengths:
   - two 12-inch (30-cm) lengths of 2 x 2 inches (5 x 5 cm)—front support posts
   - two 16-inch (40-cm) lengths of 2 x 2 inches (5 x 5 cm)—rear support posts
   - seven 4-foot (120-cm) lengths of 4 x 1¾ inches (10 x 4 cm)—front and back
   - eight 21-inch (52½-cm) lengths of 4 x 1¾ inches (10 x 4 cm)—two sides
   - two 4-foot (120-cm) lengths of 1¾ x 1 inch (4 x 2½ cm)—front and back of lid
   - three 21-inch (53-cm) lengths of 1¾ x 1 inch (4 x 2½ cm)—end and central support of lid

2. Cut down the lengths of two side pieces of wood so that 1 inch (2½ cm) is removed from the length of each. The six lengths of wood that make up the main part of each side (three per side) are screwed to the supporting posts first, so that all wood is flush, ensuring that one of the cut-down pieces is on each side. Do not worry about the excess supporting post at the rear of the cold frame.

3. Attach both the front and back lengths of wood so that they overlap the ends of the sides already in place. This will leave a box with gaps on the supporting posts on each side, but two spare 21-inch (52½-cm) lengths of 4 x 1¾ inches (10 x 4 cm). Each of these can be held up to the gaps on the sides and the sloping cut from the back of the cold frame down to the front marked for sawing. Once sawn, screw in place. Using a saw, angle the tops of the rear posts so all the pieces of wood are flush. This forms the base of the cold frame, except for handles that will be used to move it.

4. To make the handles, either cut hand-sized holes into each end if a jigsaw is handy, or attach small extra pieces from the 1¾ x 1-inch (4 x 2½-cm) wood. The latter is

done by screwing two vertical pieces into the sides; a horizontal piece of wood is then screwed in place to bridge the gap.

5. To make the lid, attach the two 4-foot (120-cm) lengths of 1¾ x 1-inch (4 x 2½-cm) wood and two of the 21-inch (53-cm) lengths of 1¾ x 1-inch (4 x 2½-cm) wood together using four of the metal angle brackets. The lid needs to be exactly the same size as the top of the cold-frame base. Attach the last 21-inch (53-cm) length of 1¾ x 1-inch (4 x 2½-cm) wood to the center of the lid using the remaining four brackets.

6. Before going any further, treat the basic framework of the cold frame with an organic wood preservative.

7. Now that the frame for the lid has been made, screw the hinges into place, with one hinge in the center of the back of the lid and the other two each 6 inches (15 cm) in from each end.

8. To attach plastic sheeting to the top of the lid, place it over the lid with about 3 inches (8 cm) overhanging all around. Cut the wood piece into four pieces to correspond to the four sides of the box. Roll the plastic around each 1 x 2-inch (2½ x 5-cm) wooden piece and nail onto the lid close to the outer edge, ensuring it is tight with no creases in it. I like to use plastic instead of glass or plexiglass because these two materials are easy to crack or break, particularly on windy days. Close the lid and screw the latch into place in the center of the lid and base.

Notes:

*   After you've made the lid of the cold frame, screw the hinges into place.

*   Wood that measures 4 x 1¾ inches (10 x 4 cm) is commonly called "two-by-four." The metric measurements are based on the actual, rather than the common, measurements.

Dibble

When planting vegetables, a trowel can be sometimes too large and cumbersome, which is when this easy-to-make dibble really comes into its own. The specifications for a homemade dibble are not precise, as I find they are usually made from whatever pieces of wood are lying around. As it is only a small tool, the cost implications of buying a larger piece of wood to cut it from make the whole project unviable. It is a very handy tool for planting leeks, bean seeds, brassica plants, and a number of transplants.

Dimensions	Materials	Tools
Size varies according to your piece of wood	Scrap piece of wood	Jigsaw Coping saw Sheet of sandpaper

Instructions

1. Cut the dibble into a "T" shape, with the vertical part about ½–1 inches (2–2½ cm) wide, preferably in both directions, and about 4 inches (10 cm) long. The horizontal part should be cut to a size that fits snugly into the palm of the person using it.

2. Once you've cut the "T" shape, rub down the whole thing with sandpaper to take off any sharp edges. Ensure that the vertical part is as round as possible. It is also useful to have the end of the vertical bit pointed to make pushing it into the ground much easier.

3. An extra that can be added is to make shallow saw cuts every ½ inch (1 cm) down the vertical part, which will help with calculating planting depths.

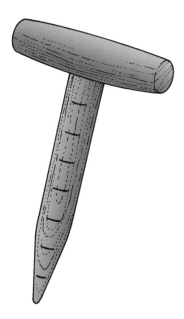

Chapter 7

A Look
at Barnsdale
Gardens

Barnsdale Gardens

The gardens at Barnsdale were initially developed from a 4-acre field by my father, gardener and television presenter Geoff Hamilton. Gradually, over a period of fourteen years, he developed this field into many small gardens for the BBC show *Gardeners' World*. The most important elements of each garden and feature were that they were relevant to the sizes and types of gardens that viewers had at home and that everything Geoff did to create and plant these areas was achievable. These principles are still very important to us today.

In 1989, our family purchased the 5½-acre adjoining plowed field, primarily to build a nursery for the propagation and sale of a wide range of plants but also to extend the amount of garden features. Since Geoff's untimely death in 1996, Barnsdale Gardens continue to develop and change as we regularly update individual gardens and features and sometimes completely change them into something new. We firmly believe that our gardens are not a tourist attraction but an education facility because the vast majority of visitors leave with at least one idea to implement in their own gardens. It is for this purpose that the gardens are open every day (except for December 24 and 25) and that their development continues under my guidance.

Following are descriptions of a selection of Barnsdale's thirty-eight distinct gardens.

The Winter Border

Originally developed during the early 1980s to highlight plants with winter interest, the border was gradually enlarged over the years until it covered quite a substantial area. In 2016, after thirty-five years, this border was in need of improvement and, fortunately, this coincided with a request from the trustees of Geoff Hamilton's New Gardeners'

Foundation charity to develop an area in the gardens to commemorate the twenty-year anniversary of Geoff's death. With a grant from the charity, the border was redeveloped for this purpose as well as to emphasize the work that has gone on in the gardens in that time. This border's main focus is still on winter, but it has been divided into smaller areas by pathways, making it more welcoming to visitors. This area also has plenty of interest throughout the other seasons of the year. Many plants in the border were donated.

The Allotment

Vegetables and fruit have always been and are still very important elements of the gardens. This garden has been enlarged over the years so it is now larger than an average allotment plot, but the produce is still grown in the same way. The plan is always to grow a wide variety of produce in smaller amounts so that we always have a lot of variety to show visitors and for us to eat. We grow many popular varieties, some rare or unusual varieties, and some that haven't yet been released by seed companies, so visitors will get to see things that are a bit different.

Japanese Garden

This area started life as a conifer bed, having been planted in 1984. However, after thirteen years, the conifers were gradually dying off from *Phytophthora* infection, a disease that attacks the stems of woody plants at ground level. This was an ideal opportunity to redevelop this bed into something completely different: a Japanese garden. Right from the beginning, this was always going to be our interpretation of a Japanese garden, not a space that stuck rigidly to the principles used in the gardens of Japan.

First, it was important to incorporate more than one style, because there are many, so we divided the garden into two halves by a water-worn, winding stone path. One side is the meditation part of the garden, where there are three standing stones arranged in a way that signifies peace and tranquility and a dry stream running to a dry pond. There is never any water in a meditation garden because it is too distracting, so we achieved the effect of water by raking the aggregate, which covers the majority of the ground, into wave patterns. The other side of the garden is heavily planted with plants originating from Japan. This side has a stream that runs into a pond that has goldfish. In the corner of this area is a bamboo tea house. To straddle the two distinct halves of the pond, and to cover the join, there is a bridge. A bridge is an essential part of a Japanese garden because it is the vantage point from which most of the garden is viewed.

The Lands' End Garden

We thought that, due to our considerable distance from the sea, it would be nice to have a garden that visitors could use as a seaside retreat. The idea was that this area would be positioned somewhere behind a line of sand dunes and used as a pit stop on the way home from a busy day at the beach. Therefore, the garden's main feature is the brightly colored beach hut that sits nicely on the decking platform. Next to the beach hut, as you would expect, are two deck chairs for unwinding and dozing. However, once hunger strikes, there is also a fire pit for barbecuing. The planting around this garden wouldn't look out of place near the sea, with trees used to create that all-important

shady area. The title of this garden relates to the clothing merchants who sponsored it, not the tip of Cornwall—although it certainly wouldn't look out of place there!

Artisan's Cottage Garden

One of two gardens built for the BBC series *Geoff Hamilton's Cottage Gardens* on a very small budget, the Artisan's Cottage Garden was designed around the old-fashioned gardener's theory that every plant will find its own best place. The plants have been positioned to tumble over the edges of the beds, softening any straight lines and making the garden feel as full of plants and color as possible. All of the features—including an arbor, tool chest, auricula theater, thyme table, and obelisk—are homemade and can be replicated easily by the average DIY enthusiast.

To make the garden feasible for all, especially those on a tight budget, most of the plants used are easy to propagate and have been self-propagated by seed, cuttings, or division. Importantly, we've used tumbling and mat-forming plants to soften and break straight edges, while the structure plants give interest all year round. One of the most exciting elements of this garden occurs in spring, when plants pop up in unexpected places.

The Gentleman's Cottage Garden

The second small garden designed and built for *Geoff Hamilton's Cottage Gardens* illustrates the perfect way to deal with an area that is wider than it is long, and the design features some of the luxuries befitting a gentleman, although it can be scaled down quite easily without losing any of the visual impact. The layout involves a central brick paver circle and four pathways leading from it that initially separate the garden into four quarters, but the clever positioning of the trellis and arches provides a fifth area, which acts as an entrance corridor. The idea is that the visitor enters through a very floriferous area and can then pass through one of the two archways leading to

either the productive fruit and vegetable beds and greenhouse on the right or the formal herb area or the plant-bordered circle of grass on the left. The handcrafted wooden love seat makes an ideal place to sit and take it all in.

The Wildlife Garden

An area that started out as the "Budget Garden" in 1984, this garden has been through several changes over the years and, in 1997, became the wildlife garden it is today. It has been designed and planted to encourage all types of wildlife not just to visit, but to stay. With this in mind, we have planted with varieties that attract as well as feed wildlife during the colder months; we also have provided habitats for mammals and mulches for insects.

The most important element, however, is a source of water. All wildlife need water to survive, and if we provide it, they won't need to go anywhere else to look for it and thus will stay right where we want them. We have positioned the small pond in the right angle of the raised patio; because the pond is not raised, visitors stand on the patio and look down into it. To give this area a bit more height and structure, we planted a *Gunnera manicata* in a large pot that stands in the water and on a shelf in the pond. The pond itself is 3 feet deep to prevent this small body of water from heating up too much in the summer and developing an algae problem.

Town Paradise Garden

One of the two gardens built for the BBC's *Geoff Hamilton's Paradise Gardens* television series, it is surrounded by high brick walls and was designed to give viewers an idea of how they could create their own little piece of paradise within an enclosed area. Although relatively expensive and technically quite difficult to build, it is a gorgeous space filled with color and scent and balanced by the tranquility of running water. The layout incorporates four beds separated by a straight path that is crisscrossed by a small stream. Each of these beds has been planted with specific varieties to make a blue and purple bed, a yellow bed, a pink and red bed, and a scented bed, making up the four.

From the lion's head fountain, set in the wall on the east side of the garden, water pours into the stream, which then empties into a pond. In front of the west-facing wall and edging the pond is a raised platform that creates the base for the handcrafted wooden gazebo. This wonderful and serene place to sit also incorporates some stunning wildlife carvings, which are a "must see" if you are visiting Barnsdale. The conservatory on the south-facing wall is the perfect place for more exotic plants and serves as a wonderful place to sit and enjoy the garden when the weather is inclement. As well as being a fabulous garden space, the Town Paradise Garden provides a wonderfully romantic setting for the many weddings at Barnsdale Gardens.

Country Paradise Garden

The less expensive of the two gardens designed and built for *Geoff Hamilton's Paradise Gardens*, this area was designed to give the feel of a woodland glade and wildflower-like perennial meadow. As with the Artisan's Cottage Garden, this space has been planted with varieties that have been self-propagated by seed, cuttings, or division. However, we did have to spend part of the budget on trees. Therefore, the arbor is made from hornbeam, while the nut walk was planted with different varieties of cobnut that was initially trained over a framework of hazel rods until the trees were tall enough to tie together at the top of each arch. The patio area at the top of the garden uses reclaimed pipes that were planted with very prostrate thymes to add extra interest and scent. The partially hidden pond is a haven for wildlife, including great crested newts.

The Herb Garden

The herb garden is a cook's dream. Created by renowned garden designer Robin Williams for a miniseries within the *Gardeners' World* television program, it is intended to be a small romantic herb feature within a larger garden. Here, plant pots and containers are used for some varieties of herb, while others are grown in pipes filled with gritty compost for excellent drainage. In this way, the pipes keep the more vigorous plants under control by containing them while also acting as an interesting retaining wall for the soil, behind which clump-forming perennials and woody herbs can be grown. The bench placed under the hop-covered arch is the perfect place to sit and take in all of the wonderful aromas.

The Ornamental Kitchen Garden

This garden was designed to incorporate flowers, fruits, and vegetables mixed in the available borders rather than grown in separate areas. At the time of its conception in 1988, this was not a new idea (in fact, this way of growing is centuries old), but this was the first time it had been brought to our television screens. There are enough beds to allow for crop rotation; a greenhouse for protected growing of fruiting vegetables, such as tomatoes and peppers; and a pergola that houses ornamental climbers and doubles as a supporting structure for the climbing vegetables. To beautify the area as well as to increase the cropping potential, we squeezed fruit varieties into every available space; therefore, visitors will find fan-trained apples, pears, red currants, and white currants; stepover apples; a lollipop apple; a wall-trained fig; and an espalier plum.

Index

Photo Credits

About the Author

Nick Hamilton is a trained horticulturist and the owner of Barnsdale Gardens, Britain's largest collection of individually designed gardens, with thirty-eight working gardens on an 8-acre site. He carries on the legacy of his father, the late Geoff Hamilton, legendary host of the BBC's *Gardener's World* TV show. Nick is the author of *The Barnsdale Handy Gardener*, *Geoff Hamilton—A Gardening Legend*, and *Grow Organic*. He has a lifelong passion and enthusiasm for organic gardening, principles that he puts into practice at Barnsdale Gardens.